THE NATION'S STAGE

The John F. Kennedy Center for the Performing Arts, 1971–2011

THE NATION'S STAGE

The John F. Kennedy Center for the Performing Arts, 1971–2011

Michael Dolan and Michael Shohl

Foreword by David M. Rubenstein and Michael M. Kaiser

Simon & Schuster
New York   London   Toronto   Sydney

A Stonesong Press Book

This book was made possible thanks to the generosity of David M. Rubenstein.

A Division of Simon & Schuster, Inc.

1230 Avenue of the Americas

New York, NY 10020

First Simon & Schuster Books edition October 2011

Produced for the John F. Kennedy Center for the Performing Arts by The Stonesong Press, LLC

Simon & Schuster and colophon are trademarks of Simon & Schuster, Inc.

Photo credits are on page 184.

For information about special discounts for bulk purchases,

please contact Simon & Schuster Special Sales at 1-866-218-3049 or visit our website at *www.simonspeakers.com*.

Designers: Chris Lorette David, Sophia Latto

Produced by The Stonesong Press

Manufactured in the United States of America

10 9 8 7 6 5 4 3 2 1

Library of Congress Cataloging-in-Publication Data

Dolan, Michael, 1955-

  The nation's stage : the John F. Kennedy Center for the Performing Arts, 1971-2011 / Michael Dolan.

      p. cm.

  Includes bibliographical references.

1. John F. Kennedy Center for the Performing Arts (U.S.) I. Title. II. Title: John F. Kennedy Center for the Performing Arts, 1971-2011.

  PN1588.W3D55 2011

  792.509753--dc23

2011017025

ISBN HC: 9781451629446

ISBN TP: 9781451635256

ISBN Special Edition HC: 9781451635249

TABLE OF CONTENTS

FOREWORD

Since its opening in 1971, the John F. Kennedy Center for the Performing Arts has emerged as one of the world's most important, exciting, and respected centers for the performing arts. With more than 2,000 performances each season, an education program that serves eleven million Americans annually, and an arts management training program that has taught arts leaders from seventy-two nations, it is one of the busiest arts venues in the world.

This level of achievement could not have been easily predicted. Enacting federal legislation to create a national cultural center took several decades. The final authorization in 1958 came with no federal appropriation. The initial efforts to raise the requisite private funds for construction went poorly. And the nation's capital, for all of its other virtues, was not well-known for its commitment to, or interest in, the performing arts.

So what happened over the past four decades to make this Center, re-authorized in 1964 as a living memorial to President Kennedy, such an indispensable part of life in Washington and such a vibrant force in the performing arts world?

The answer: the long-time support and active involvement of a great many dedicated, visionary, and committed individuals who saw the potential of a national cultural center.

For forty years, presidents, cabinet members, and members of Congress have faithfully supported the Center and attended its performances.

Over the same period, members of President Kennedy's family, in particular Senator Edward Kennedy, Ambassador Jean Kennedy Smith, and Caroline Kennedy, devoted considerable time and effort to ensuring that the Center would meet and exceed the goals established by Congress.

Roger Stevens, who spent nearly three decades as the Board of Directors' first chairman, made certain through his inspired and intense hands-on involvement that the Center had no choice but to succeed. Those who followed Roger in that role—Ralph P. Davidson, James D. Wolfensohn, James A. Johnson, and Stephen A. Schwarzman—made their own distinctive and important contributions to the Center's health and vitality.

These chairs have been aided immeasurably by the members of Congress and scores of citizens from throughout the country who, once appointed by a president of the United States, have served as trustees.

Thousands of full-time employees and volunteers at the Center have brought the dedication needed to build and maintain a world-class performing arts center.

And, of course, the Kennedy Center has been blessed from its start with performances of the world's most significant and talented artists and the efforts of the finest art educators.

Yet the work of all of these vital people would not have been enough without the support of the Kennedy Center's loyal patrons. Their support, through ticket sales and contributions, has enabled the Kennedy Center to operate at a level unimaginable forty years ago.

The pages that follow celebrate, commemorate, and display only a fraction of the arts performances and educational initiatives that have both contributed to the Center's vibrancy and been nourished by its support. We hope you enjoy this look at *The Nation's Stage*: your stage, in every sense, for so many Americans have supported, built, and contributed to this thriving national cultural center for these United States. The Nation's Stage belongs to all of us.

— *David M. Rubenstein and Michael M. Kaiser*

DAVID M. RUBENSTEIN became Chairman of the John F. Kennedy Center for the Performing Arts in May 2010. MICHAEL M. KAISER has been Kennedy Center President since 2001.

The Concert Hall, opened in 1971 and renovated in 1997, is the most spacious performance venue in the Kennedy Center, seating 2,454.

INTRODUCTION

> "There is a connection, hard to explain logically but easy to feel, between achievement in public life and progress in the arts. The age of Pericles was also the age of Phidias. The age of Lorenzo de Medici was also the age of Leonardo da Vinci. The age of Elizabeth was also the age of Shakespeare, and the new frontier for which I campaign in public life can also be a new frontier for American art."
>
> —John F. Kennedy

To stand before the John F. Kennedy Center for the Performing Arts is an awe-inspiring experience. The building is 630 feet long, a distance of two football fields, end to end. It is over 100 feet high, eclipsing the height of the Sphinx by thirty feet. It is 300 feet wide, equivalent to a thirty-story building. The exterior walls are covered with 3,700 tons of Carrara marble. The Grand Foyer is one of the largest rooms in the world and is 75 feet longer than the Washington Monument is high.

But the Center is far more than marble and stone and metal. It represents a country's belief in the power and importance of the arts. A nation's devotion to commerce will promote stability. A nation's emphasis on defense will promote security.

But a nation's commitment to the arts will encourage passion, inspiration, and imagination.

The Center isn't just about entertainment. In addition to offering a variety of artistic expressions for viewers to enjoy, it also offers the arts as a form of education, bringing theater, music, dance, and more from around the nation and around the globe to patrons old and young, to aficionados and to those who've never seen such works, and offering both students and professionals alike lessons in ballet, classical music, voice, and much more. Kennedy Center programs teach skills, discipline, commitment, teamwork, and a kind of faith that all of these strengths can be used to create something truly amazing.

The Beginning

The institution that became the John F. Kennedy Center for the Performing Arts was conceived amid excitement and anxiety. In 1958, when President Dwight D. Eisenhower signed the National Cultural Center Act, authorizing construction of such a building in Washington, D.C., the United States was enjoying unparalleled prosperity. At the same time, the Cold War was intensifying. The arts were tangled in that tension.

Apart from local philanthropists such as the Ford and Guggenheim Foundations, subsidies for the arts were scarce in the United States. At the national level, funding was all but invisible. When President Eisenhower signed the national cultural center into law, it was the first time that the federal government had put tax dollars toward constructing a structure dedicated to the performing arts.

The splendid Grand Foyer of the Kennedy Center, one of the largest rooms in the world, is lit by sixteen chandeliers and wall sconces of Orrefors crystal, gifts from Sweden.

At the time, America's artistic focus seemed to tend more toward crowd-pleasing fare. Americans were more drawn to Hollywood blockbusters and chart-topping music hits, not to the classical forms. There seemed more of an interest in "pop culture" than in "culture."

In mandating the Center, Congress set what seemed to be a reasonable annual sum of federal support and decreed that, once the building was up, the National Park Service would maintain it. Authorization in hand, officials analyzed seven sites around Washington, D.C. In time, the search committee eliminated all the sites except a patch of Foggy Bottom opposite Theodore Roosevelt Island. The acquisition required complex negotiations involving the White House, the U.S. Navy, the Department of the Interior, and the Board of Commissioners of the District of Columbia. Officials hired architect Edward Durell Stone, designer of the U.S. Embassy in New Delhi and codesigner of New York's Museum of Modern Art. Stone drew a flowerlike structure, 100

feet tall and 180 feet in diameter, which he said would cost about $75 million. The Center's trustees nodded and went to work raising money. It wouldn't be as easy as they hoped.

The Eisenhower Theater's 2008 renovation enhanced both its intimacy and technical capabilities.

President Kennedy

During the 1960 election, John F. Kennedy campaigned with the slogan "Let's get America moving again." Some people can still recall hearing him say that in his Boston bark, fuzzed by AM radio static. In person and through the megaphone of the media, the young senator had an invigorating effect.

Among people Kennedy moved was Spain's Pablo Casals, widely regarded as the world's most talented cellist. Casals had been a master musician a long time. After exiling himself from his homeland to protest Franco's takeover, and living in Puerto Rico, Casals heard something in Kennedy's presidential campaign he found inspiring. He wrote to the candidate wishing him success. Kennedy wrote back. An epistolary friendship bloomed.

After taking office, Kennedy invited Casals to play in the East Room again. The occasion was a state dinner honoring Puerto Rico's governor, Luis Muñoz-Marín. The day of the event, November 13, 1961, the President met with Casals. That evening, the Kennedys dined with their guests and then repaired to the East Room. There, Casals favored the group with a few classical pieces, climaxing with an encore of "Song of the Birds," the Catalan folk song with which he

Architect Edward Durell Stone (second from right) shows President Kennedy (center) an early model of one of his designs for the Kennedy Center.

had closed every appearance since going into exile, and which embodied his yearning for freedom.

That concert, which drew worldwide attention, became a highlight among many touchstones of the Kennedy cultural legacy, including poet Robert Frost's reading at Kennedy's inauguration, African-American mezzo-soprano Grace Bumbry's 1962 East Room performance, and a host of other associations linking the Kennedy presidency to the arts.

Also in 1961, and also at Kennedy's request, another man of prominence visited the White House. The president wanted to ask if real estate mogul and Broadway producer Roger L. Stevens would chair the cultural center project. Stevens, who had made a mark raising money for Adlai Stevenson, said he'd take the job with the condition that the government covered his expenses, paid him one dollar a year, and provided a car and driver when he was in the capital. The men shook on it. Stevens went to work. To improve fund-raising, he organized *An American Pageant for the Arts*, a closed-circuit TV spectacular. Aired at locations in 150 cities on November 29, 1962, the program starred the President and Mrs. Kennedy, with an appearance by former president Eisenhower and performances by Marian Anderson, Harry Belafonte, Fredric March, Bob Newhart, and seven-year-old cello prodigy Yo-Yo Ma. Despite the impressive artistic display, ticket sales enlarged the building fund by less than $500,000. Another fund-raiser, a coffee-table book with text by Frost, James Baldwin, and other celebrated American writers, did no better. A benefit record of performances by the service bands sold well, but not *that* well.

Adjustments were in order. Stevens studied Stone's plans. Concluding that the floral design could cost $100 million to construct, he asked the architect to return to the drawing board. Stone brought back a simpler rectangular scheme he said would offer "idyllic repose in one of the most glorious settings in the world." It also would cost far less to build, doubtless a factor in a congressional decision to give the trustees five more years to raise the money.

In his efforts on behalf of the national cultural center, the president didn't stop at television appearances. In October 1963, he invited a roomful of American CEOs to lunch and asked that a hundred companies each contribute $100,000 toward the center. "The nations of the world have their great and beautiful centers for the performing arts, but here in the world's greatest capital we have nothing," Kennedy said. The CEOs agreed to help fill that gap.

The corporations' largesse was to be announced early in 1964 at a White House dinner. But before then, in late November 1963, the president and Mrs. Kennedy flew to Dallas for what was supposed to be a standard political fence-mending trip, but ended in Kennedy's tragic assassination.

Within days of the event, discussion began of how to honor the slain president, perhaps by renaming Pennsylvania Avenue. Instead, the project on Roger Stevens's plate became the John F. Kennedy Center for the Performing Arts. Besides advancing the arts in America and the world, the Center would serve as Kennedy's sole official memorial in

the capital. Congress agreed to fund the difference between the cost of building the Center and $12 million the trustees had amassed.

During groundbreaking on December 2, 1964, President Lyndon Johnson turned up the first earth with a gold-plated shovel, a tool of considerable pedigree. President McKinley used it in 1898 in a White House tree planting. In 1914, President Taft broke ground with it for the Lincoln Memorial. In 1938, President Franklin D. Roosevelt did the same for the Jefferson Memorial.

By 1965, volunteers calling themselves the Friends of the Kennedy Center were giving hard-hat tours of the construction site. They also gave slide shows at business meetings and schools and staffed a trailer, located a little inland of where the Hall of Nations is, in which visiting dignitaries could study a model of the building. They organized the Tom Sawyer Project, which had schoolchildren paint panels to decorate the safety fences ringing the excavation. (A little more than fifteen years later, the volunteer Friends of the Kennedy Center numbered nearly seven thousand, including a core of several hundred members who regularly stood watch to give tours and staff an information booth and the gift shop that replaced the card table and cigar box of the 1960s. By 2011, their more than eighty-five thousand hours yearly of voluntary work amounted to a million and a half dollars in labor.)

In 1966, Jacqueline Kennedy commissioned composer Leonard Bernstein to write a piece of music to be performed at the dedication. Three years later, one of the Center's earliest programs, the American College Theater Festival, began in tents on the Mall, later moving to Ford's Theatre in downtown Washington.

Construction was supposed to take two to three years; it took more than six. When jets began using National Airport, the roof and windows had to be reworked

President Lyndon Johnson breaks ground for the Center in December 1964. Robert F. Kennedy, the late president's brother, (back center) looks on.

Left: Roger Stevens (left) with Patrick Hayes and Aldus Chapin, managing director and vice president of the Washington Performing Arts Society, respectively, on a hardhat tour of the construction of the Center.

Above: The Kennedy Center, quick to include the surrounding community from the beginning, and with the help of the Friends of the Kennedy Center, created the Tom Sawyer project, which asked each state to provide safety panels, painted by the children, to help brighten the construction zone and bring beauty to the Center prior to its completion.

Unexpected Dividend

I've been volunteering at the Kennedy Center since before there was a Kennedy Center. I've worked every Tuesday since 1968. I was with the Service Guild of Washington, which did volunteer work all over the city. I called Lily Guest at the Center and asked if she could use some volunteers. She said to come to a trailer that stood a little inland of where the Hall of Nations is. There were twelve of us. We'd give tours of the site in hard hats. To promote the Friends of the Kennedy Center, we ran a speakers bureau, taking a slide show to business meetings and schools. I've always been a tour guide.

When the Center opened, everybody wanted to see it. We'd each take a position, wait for a few hundred people to gather, and then give the spiel. Eventually more volunteers signed up, and we could take groups of fifty or so on real tours.

I never expected when I started volunteering at the Center that I'd be there for forty-three years, or that I'd have a grandson who'd spend two years as a fellow with the National Symphony Orchestra. His name is Daniel Getz. He plays the viola. In 2008, my fortieth anniversary as a volunteer, I came to the annual volunteers gala, and there was Daniel to play for me.

—Geri Lewis

GERI LEWIS is the longest-serving Kennedy Center volunteer.

to block the noise. Structural steel cost millions more than estimated. A strike in Italy delayed delivery of a load of donated Carrara marble. These and other bumps delayed the opening several times. On certain aspects the planners missed the mark by a wide margin. They assumed there would be only a two-member staff—the chairman and a secretary. And they included no rehearsal space.

However, the Center did open, and it would be supported by strangers and family alike, far and near. Twenty-two African nations contributed gifts to establish the African Lounge. Sweden and Norway contributed chandeliers, to the Grand Foyer and Opera House, respectively. Both Edward M. Kennedy and Jean Kennedy Smith would serve on the Kennedy Center Board of Directors, both striving to maintain the family's vision of what the Center should be. Room was found for offices and rehearsals. An array of programs began to blossom. Some took familiar routes while others lit out for unexplored territories or sought new angles on the familiar. From the National Symphony Orchestra (NSO) to the Washington National Opera (WNO) to The Suzanne Farrell Ballet to the battalions of performers who have appeared at the Center, all have the same goal: artistic excellence. Striving to present artists and performances of the highest caliber, the Center illuminates culture, showing how and why the arts matter, in the United States and around the world.

Always Evolving

As the arts evolve, so does the Center. Decade to decade, it has reengineered programming and emphasis and even quotidian elements such as transportation, aiming continually to strengthen the ties that bind a unique entity to the world, to the nation, and to its hometown of Washington, D.C.

The effect is to reflect the spirit of a country and a culture directed ever forward. The Kennedy Center was no more finished in 1971 or in 2011 than the United States was finished in 1787 or in

1865. As Americans have labored to keep perfecting their union and to maintain its place in a world that refuses to stand still, the Center has adapted to the resulting changes. In the words of Center president Michael M. Kaiser, "There's a new Kennedy Center every five years." Viewed over the long haul, the Center calendar charts signal advances in American life.

Even if that masterwork had been available, the Kennedy Center of 1971 would not have staged August Wilson's 20th Century, a festival celebrating the playwright's life and work, but in 2008 the Kennedy Center did stage all ten Wilson plays, to great acclaim.

In 1971, few Americans could even conceive of personal computers, never mind personal computers behaving like TV sets that could show live performances, but since 1998 Millennium Stage has employed technology to do exactly that.

For many Americans in 1971, China was an enigma and the Arab world was mostly ignored, but in 2005 and 2009 Kennedy Center festivals celebrating

The Center's renowned celebrations have included the month-long August Wilson's 20th Century *(2007), performances of Wilson's ten plays, each exploring the African-American experience in a different decade.*

The African Lounge, created with gifts from twenty-two African nations, is decorated with artwork that represents traditional styles and designs passed down through generations.

The KC Jazz Club in the roof-level Terrace Gallery is home to performances by jazz veterans and fresh, contemporary talent.

those cultures drew record crowds and earned well-deserved plaudits.

The arts foster connections, both obvious and subtle, that make the world more intimate, even in troubled times, and in that process the Center operates at the vanguard. Each season brings extraordinary moments, many of them pictured in these pages. In addition to appearances by the greatest names in the arts, the Center also shines a spotlight on rising young performers, as well as talents from around the world who may or may not achieve the fame their artistry deserves but who strive to preserve, perfect, and present it anyway.

Not every innovation or development at the Center led to ideal results. Like a play, or a piece of music, the processes of composition sometimes requires editing, requires the addition of something that might have been omitted or the substitution of something that doesn't quite fit. This was seen during the attempt to establish a national theater under Peter Sellars, an earnest experiment that had some uneven results. The very effort to bring the Center into existence included arrangements

that time revealed as unsatisfactory, such as having the Park Service manage the building and grounds.

The Sellars years ended early. Congressional amendments in 1994 corrected fiscal and managerial imbalances and set the stage for renovations to render the building barrier-free, an overdue chord in the Kennedyesque theme of freedom. The same decade saw a small but significant tightening of the bonds between Center and city—the start of free shuttle service between the Center and Washington's subway system, encouraging use of public transportation and making the Center more accessible.

A broadcast presence that began with televised concerts expanded to include popular prime-time programs that chronicle the awarding of the Kennedy Center Honors and the Mark Twain Prize for American Humor, as well as a National Public Radio jazz series. All these have brought the Center into millions of households, as has online content streamed directly to a computer, tablet, or smart phone.

In addition to serving as a place to showcase amazing performances and

artistic contributions, the Center has also served as a platform for education. The performing arts don't merely entertain, they also teach us about what we hold dear, who we are, what moves us, what inspires us. The arts are a moving, shifting history. With that in mind, the Center has served as a dynamic resource for education, not only teaching young people music, dance, and theater, but also teaching us about our own history and culture.

The Center is nothing if not flexible. In the early days, Roger Stevens had the standing and the good sense to invite the American Film Institute (AFI) aboard. AFI stayed many years, occupying offices and operating a movie house. When the AFI moved out, its space reemerged as the popular Family Theater. The closing of the Library of Congress reading room on the Terrace level inspired the opening of the Jazz Club, adding another facet to the Center's support of that American art form. An informal arrangement that began nearly thirty years ago with a handful of college interns working in Center offices has grown to become the

Lily Tomlin accepts the 2003 Mark Twain Prize, named for the fearless humorist and observer of nineteenth-century American society whose uncompromising perspectives on social and personal folly startle and delight readers to this day. The comic talents of Twain Prize recipients often do the same.

DeVos Institute for Arts Management at the Kennedy Center. The DeVos Institute's fellowship, capacity building, and internship programs set the global standard for educational and professional advancement in its field.

Much has happened in forty years. Eras and tenures overlap, influences intertwine and contrast and compete, personalities and purviews and interests meld and separate. In the end, there are the performances, grand and compact and all points between, collections of moments that exist on stages and reverberate inside the lives of those who experience them, who execute them, who plan them, and who conceive them. Again and again, the Center has responded to its times by making the most of

them, and by summoning the best from those who serve it. After the incomparable Stevens retired, the roles of the board of trustees, the board chairman, and the chief executive had the chance to flourish, and did. From the trustees and leaders who guide it to the workforce that performs, stages, administers, cleans, repairs, patrols, and feeds, among many other tasks, to the volunteer brigades that facilitate its operations and the audiences that fill its seats and halls, this village of the performing arts enters its fifth decade with an exuberance matched only by its

dedication and its intentions of rivaling and outdoing the considerable achievements of its first four decades.

Above: *An overhead view of the Center during construction reveals its ambitious scale.*

Right: *The Center's stunning location on the Potomac has allowed inventive programming, from Cao Guo-Qiang's 2005 Tornado fireworks spectacular over the river to conceptual artist Jenny Holzer's projections of presidential quotes onto Roosevelt Island in 2007.*

Alan Titus (center) performs with the Alvin Ailey American Dance Theater in Bernstein's Mass. *Ailey choreographed the piece.*

I. THE THEATER OF THE OPENING, THE OPENING OF THE THEATER

On September 8, 1971, the Center was dedicated. After Roger Stevens offered a brief welcome, the Opera House curtains opened on the world premiere of Leonard Bernstein's *Mass: A Theatre Piece for Singers, Players and Dancers*. Based on the Latin rite the Roman Catholic Church used until the reforms of Vatican II, *Mass* incorporated English-language texts by Bernstein, Broadway composer Stephen Schwartz, and singer-songwriter Paul Simon.

With its performing complement of two hundred and a celebrity-dense audience, the Bernstein premiere glittered like the night's oversized gilt tickets. The souvenir program, published by Saturday Review Press, included a touching prose poem about John F. Kennedy by Alan Jay Lerner and an extended-play seven inch record.

The next evening, with President and Mrs. Nixon in attendance, Antal Doráti and the National Symphony Orchestra christened the Concert Hall. Simon Estes sang "Secular Cantata No. 2, a Free Song," a new piece by American composer William Schuman. Isaac Stern soloed on Mozart's Violin Concerto No. 3 in G Major. The Orchestra performed Stravinsky's "Rite of Spring" and Beethoven's overture to The Consecration of the House, op. 124.

The poster for Leonard Bernstein's Mass: A Theatre Piece for Singers, Players and Dancers *introduced the Center's first performance, which lasted two hours and included a cast of 200.*

The Center was an instant sensation. There was a full schedule of performers and performances, but the shows were only part of the extravaganza. Even before the opening, visitors thronged, overrunning the volunteers. Tour guides didn't need hard-hats now; they needed bullhorns. Instead of trying to lead anyone anywhere, Friends would stake out spots along a prearranged route throughout the building. Each would wait for a few hundred onlookers to gather and then begin that portion of the presentation. The commentary might quantify the scale of the Grand Foyer. Or visitors might learn that the building's decorative fixtures, such as chandeliers, mirrors, and stage curtains, were donated by more than forty nations. They would discover that Robert Berks's bronze bust of John F. Kennedy weighed three thousand pounds. They would be amazed by

Jacqueline Kennedy attends an early performance at the Center, with Roger Stevens (on her left) and Leonard Bernstein (bottom left).

the capacities of the three theaters, that the Eisenhower Theater, named for the president who signed the Center into existence, could hold 1,122; the Opera House, 2,294; the Concert Hall 2,454. Once done talking, that Friend would direct the crowd to the next Friend, and so on. As the mob scene faded and more volunteers signed on, regular guided tours began and continue today.

The Age of Stevens

Between 1961, when his president called him to service, and 1988, when he retired, Roger Stevens was the Center's *genius loci* and benevolent general—roles for which prowess in business, show, and otherwise, uniquely equipped him.

Through the troubled early days and the dark passage after Dallas, Stevens stayed the course. He worked with the White House and Congress to bring the Center into being. He raised and contributed money and persuaded others to do the same. He served on a committee organized to define the Center's mission whose ranks included Jacqueline Kennedy. That panel, also assigned to choose a chairman and chief executive

officer, named a general director, former Ambassador William McCormick Blair. However, Stevens made clear that he meant to run the place. Blair wore the mantle. Stevens held the reins.

Stevens became a presence in the capital. That status enlarged once he could don a hard hat and patrol his riverside domain as the building rose. He and his staff operated downtown—naturally, in offices he wrangled—until they could occupy workspace carved into a region behind the Eisenhower Theater. The door to his windowless office was always open.

It was said of Roger Stevens that he never met a playwright he didn't like, and Roger Stevens met a lot of playwrights. Stevens had been recruited for the Center in large part because of his success as a Broadway producer, so it was not surprising that theater would occupy a very important aspect of the Center for the chairman. During his tenure at the Center, he ran the theatrical show, period. Programming developed energetically in other areas, but the schedule tilted toward the boss's keenest interest.

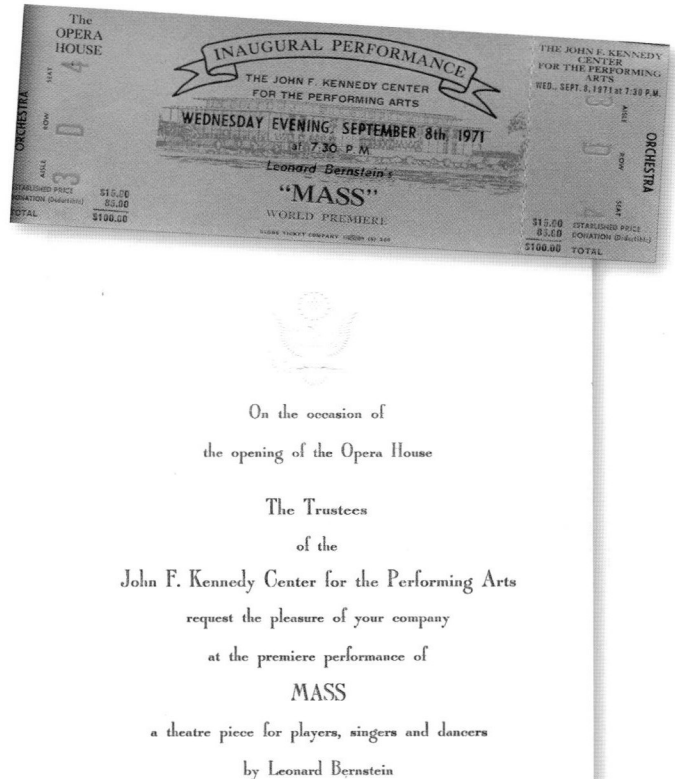

Top: *Opening Night Ticket*

Bottom: *Black Tie Invitation to the Opening Night*

The Man To See

He was shy, a Midwesterner who came East to do well and did much, much better, making fortunes in real estate and, more than once, on Broadway.

A real estate man's son, he was a teenage whiz at bridge, blackjack, and poker. Choate let him graduate even though business failures impoverished his family midway through his senior year. Harvard accepted him, but the Depression deflected him to the University of Michigan, and after a year, he dropped out. He moved home to Detroit, where he lived in rooming houses, selling the occasional pint of blood to get by. He worked on a Ford assembly line and pumped gas. He educated himself at the public library.

In the mid-1930s he went into real estate and, by 1937, he was making $25,000 a year and had $50,000 in the bank. He said the Depression was the best thing that ever happened to him.

During World War II, even though he'd dropped out of college, he persuaded the Navy to give him a commission. He spent the duration with a unit responsible for maintaining oxygen equipment in Miami, Florida. After the war he bought hotels there. Later, in New York City, his interest in theater blossomed, and he managed the Actor's Studio.

In 1951, he organized a syndicate that bought the Empire State Building. To ensure a smooth closing, the principals held a dress rehearsal. At the end of the actual event, all present broke into applause. He said he'd never heard anything like it except on an opening night.

Roger Stevens sits in the driver's seat on a bulldozer during the 1965 groundbreaking construction in this playful publicity photo; his legendary energy helped drive the construction of the Center at this time.

At times he had as many as fifteen plays running in which he had a hand. One of the most impressive characters of the theatrical world, he mumbled, a touch of Runyon that could cut with startling illumination to the matter at hand. You could imagine him shoving a hand under Nathan Detroit's chin to ask the color of that day's cravat.

In 1961, President Kennedy asked him to get a national cultural center off the ground. He spent a decade doing that, and then spent much of the next two running the place. He was not only its founder but also its impresario, its angel, its artistic conscience.

He was the first chairman of the National Endowment for the Arts. He won a Tony. At the Center, he regularly took shifts as a theater monitor, patrolling the aisles and halls to see that all was well, and that all remained so.

Asked why he'd brought the National Symphony Orchestra beneath the Kennedy Center rubric, he said, "What's a city, especially our nation's capital, without a symphony orchestra?" Pressed as to the nuances of overhead and governance, he added with a magisterial wave, "Ahhh, it'll work out." Sometimes, when a show didn't cover its costs, he covered the spread.

Though tenderhearted, he could be gruff. Colleague Martin Feinstein once took him aside to explain that a member of Feinstein's staff had said she believed he thought her name to be "God damn it, Judy."

On a deal-hunting trip to Manhattan, the Center's attorney accompanied him. Deep in the Shubert Organization warren, he and a panjandrum of the business came to terms over a production. They stood to shake on it. The lawyer said he'd draw up a contract.

"Young man," the fellow from Shubert said, incredulous, "I just shook hands with Roger Stevens. That is a contract."

Glory Days

Appearing at the Kennedy Center during the great Roger Stevens's time was always a feather in one's cap. You'd be up in New York and mention that you were going to play the Center, and everyone's eyes would light up and they'd say how lucky you were. It was a wonderful gig. We old-timers always talk about the glory days, and those were glory days. It was a very special time, and the Center had a wonderful atmosphere. Still does, I'm sure. I feel very gratified to have worked there.

—Rosemary Harris

ROSEMARY HARRIS, a participant in the Center's 2004 "Women in Tennessee" symposium with Zoe Caldwell, Estelle Parsons, and Eva Marie Saint, appeared at the Center in *Royal Family*, *Old Times*, *Hay Fever*, and *Home and Beauty*.

Among key Stevens hires was Martin Feinstein, who as executive director booked dance and music and organized festivals; in effect, that which was not theater was his to handle. Feinstein, who had developed his considerable skills as a promoter, manager, and negotiator working for the impresario Sol Hurok, brought to his tasks at the Center encyclopedic knowledge of the arts as well as a dynamic personality that dovetailed with Stevens's famous reserve.

The early Stevens years included the assembly of a board of directors appointed by the President of the United States—a system unique to the Center. Membership ranged far and wide, and included members of the political elite, but the citizenry of Washington, D.C., was also well represented, on the theory that area residents would be the main beneficiaries and so ought to be the main benefactors of the Center.

For decades the National Symphony Orchestra had played Constitution Hall. While it may have been a fine room in which to convene meetings for the Daughters of the American Revolution or have The Who open for Herman's Hermits, in terms of orchestral acoustics, it was no prize. When local impresarios booked prestige talent like Dame Margot Fonteyn and Rudolf Nureyev, they sometimes had to stage the ballets at the Washington Coliseum, where customary fare was hockey games, wrestling matches, and rock 'n' roll shows. Washingtonians were eager for a genuine cultural hub.

However, culture costs dearly, and in Washington big givers were in short supply. Often a municipality's corporate citizens carry much local philanthropic weight. Washington, being a center of government, had few large private enterprises to call its own. Big companies with offices in the capital might write a few checks to charity, but the real money went to arts organizations in the local community where the company had its headquarters. That meant an uphill march to obtain private financial support at the local Washington, D.C., level. So Stevens formed the Community and Friends Board, which reflected the metropolitan area in its membership and outlook. The goal was to bring the Center into closer

Andrea McArdle onstage at the Kennedy Center stars as the lead in the original 1977 pre-Broadway production of Annie. *For her work, she became the youngest actor to receive a Tony Award nomination.*

contact with the community and create local advocates.

Risks and Rewards

Theater is a matter of moments. Sometimes the moment is literally that—an actor delivers a line, and the world turns upside down. Theater can be incredibly personal, a dramatic universe occupied by a single performer delivering a moving soliloquy. It can also be a tremendous spectacle, as the crowd holds its breath, the houselights dim, the curtain hitches up oh so slowly, and what look like a thousand dancing feet make thunder. Sometimes the moment defies gravity and the clock, even the calendar.

Through the decades, the Center has had a hand in the production of more than three hundred new theatrical vehicles, including Tony-winning shows. Notable productions include *Annie, Les Misérables* (which had its U.S. premiere at the Center), *A Few Good Men, First Monday in October, Jumpers, Mass, Medea, On Your Toes, Pippin, Ragtime, The Royal Family, Wings, The Little Foxes,* and *You Can't Take it With You.*

Elizabeth Taylor graces the stage as Regina. She appeared in the role in the 1981 revival of Lillian Hellman's The Little Foxes *at the Center.*

The celebrated Broadway musical production of Les Misérables *appeared at the Kennedy Center's Opera House in its out-of-town tryout from December 1986 to February 1987, before opening in New York. The 1988 cast is shown here.*

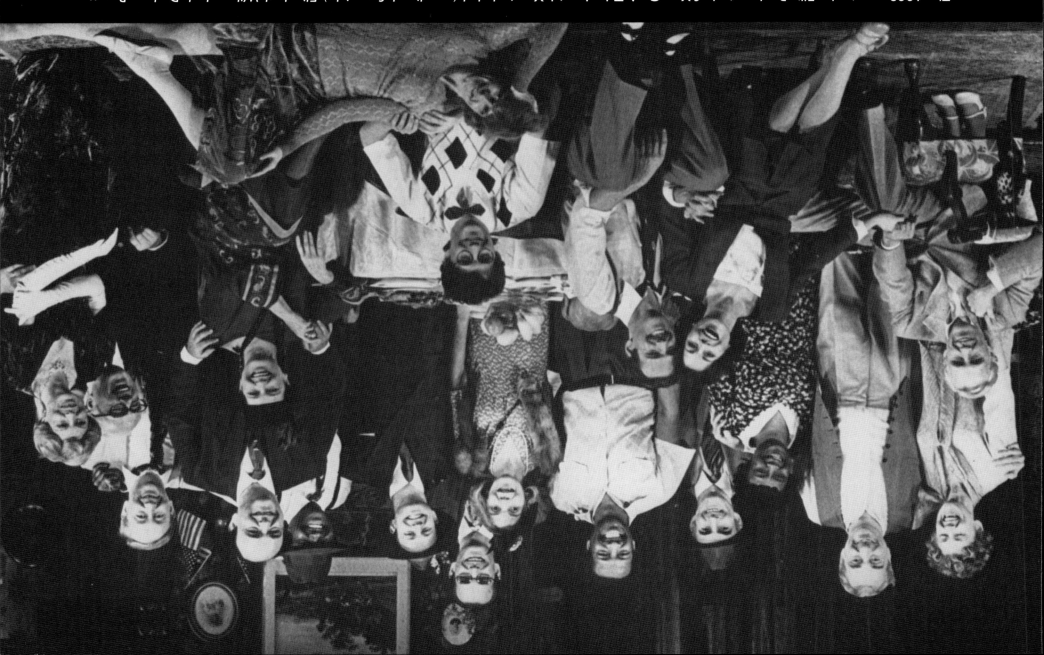

The 1983 cast in the Ellis Rabb revival of You Can't Take It with You included (standing, left to right) Elizabeth Wilson, Jack Dodson, Rosetta Le Noire, Maureen Anderman, Nicolas Surovy, Christopher Foster, Colleen Dewhurst, Lawrence Weber, Meg Mundy; (front, lying down) Carol Androsky, Jason Robards, Page Johnson, Arthur French, Alice Drummond, Orrin Reiley, William Castleman, Wayne Elbert, James Coco, Bill McCutcheon; (seated, left to right)

As the Center's founding theatrical spirit, Roger Stevens set an adventuresome course. To Stevens, who was producing on Broadway when a national performing arts center was barely a concept, risk went with reward.

The Center produced. The Center coproduced. The Center underwrote and subsidized and took investment shares in exchange for shots at success. The Center welcomed rentals, national touring companies, and out-of-town tryouts. If it was theater and it wanted to play in Washington, D.C., it had a chance of doing so here.

In the beginning there was the Eisenhower Theater and the Opera House. Stevens conveyed to the design team that he meant the Eisenhower to replicate the feel of Manhattan's old Helen Hayes Theater, a Forty-sixth Street institution. The Opera House, of course, would be for opera and ballet but also for ambitious plays capable of making the most out of a larger stage. But those are only two of the Center's many theaters.

Theater abhors a vacuum. Six stories up, on the Terrace level, open space beckoned, and soon stages grew there.

In 1977, the Musical Theater Lab, a joint project between the Center and the Stuart Ostrow Foundation, took form in the middle ground behind the Atrium—a space originally designed for convention gatherings. The Lab was a pioneering effort to "workshop" new musicals. To encourage audiences and contain costs, Roger Stevens negotiated with unions for an exemption from salary requirements. In exchange, admission was free. Energetic producers including Ostrow, Ted Chapin, and Scott Rudin put on envelope-pushing productions such as Ostrow's *The Robber Bridegroom*, based on Eudora Welty's 1942 novella and starring Patti LuPone, *Up On the Mountain*, directed by George Faison, and Arthur Miller's *Up From Paradise*, directed by Dan Sullivan. Other Musical Theater Lab projects included *Joe's Opera*, *The Red Blue-Grass Western Flyer Show*, *King Arthur's Tales*, *Saints*, *Hot Grog*, *Neverland*, and *Amerika*.

Also during the 1970s, the Terrace-level Atrium housed the Chautauqua Tent, whose name and function harkened to the original edutainment: summer programs of theater, music, and

---

The American People Have Decided

The perception around the country is, okay, we might not have an official national theater, but the Kennedy Center is it. We tour a lot, and I hear that from people all over. As far as they're concerned, there's Broadway, and there's the Kennedy Center. That's what the American people have decided. And let me tell you, playing the Kennedy Center really impresses your parents back in Texas.

—Jaston Williams

JASTON WILLIAMS, coauthor and costar with Joe Sears of the widely honored plays *Greater Tuna*, *A Tuna Christmas*, *Red White and Tuna*, and *Tuna Does Vegas*, received the L.A. Dramalogue Award for *Greater Tuna* and *A Tuna Christmas*.

Broadway touring productions frequently come to the Center. The musical Hairspray was in the Opera House in summer 2005; here the Dynamites perform the colorful "Welcome to the 60s" number.

lectures that started in upstate New York in 1874, spread nationwide, and lasted until the 1920s, when radio did them in. The Chautauqua Tent, part of the Center's celebration of the Bicentennial, was a revival of the communitarian ideal. The Tent was the scene of exhibits and performance series such as *America on Stage*, which in 1975–76 welcomed appearances by community theater companies from around the country.

Stages Sprouting Through a New Decade

Theater at the Center continued to develop in unexpected directions and places through the 1980s. In 1987, *Shear Madness*, a raucous farce set in a beauty parlor, took root in the Theater Lab, where its brand of participatory comedy still rules. The remaining fallow hours prompted a swing-shift arrangement. Crews swapped around sets so children's theater shows could make

The original 1987 cast of the wildly successful Shear Madness *pose with the show's creators, Bruce Jordan (lower left) and Marilyn Abrams (second left), who also starred in the production.*

use of the space when the beauty shop of *Madness* wasn't bopping. Later, when the Family Theater opened, children's shows moved downstairs. The college theater festival and other education presentations gravitated to fill in around *Shear Madness*.

Still running strong, the raucous comedy has become a full-fledged theatrical wonder in Washington and many other markets. As of December 31, 2010, the local production, through whose cast some 250 actors have passed, had logged 10,260 performances seen by 2,850,000 people, nearly thirty-two percent of the nine million who have seen the show worldwide. Many of those local millions enjoyed *Shear Madness* as teenagers experiencing their first brush with live theater, just as the NSO's Concerts for Young People have provided an introduction for millions to classical music, albeit without slapstick or beauty products.

Taking Theater on the Road

Stevens wasn't content to simply use the Center as a stage for the arts in the nation's capital. He saw the Kennedy Center as an opportunity to bring theater to the rest of the country. One of the ways Stevens hoped to share his love of theater with the community, and beyond, was by establishing the Kennedy Center American College Theater festival. The Festival presents a year-round series of state, regional, and national events. More than nine hundred college and university theater departments nationwide participate in the program. Yearly in January and February, eight regional festivals host young actors, playwrights, directors, designers, and critics, who participate for three to five days of workshops, symposia, and performances. Outstanding students are recognized with scholarships and opportunities to study and work at the Sundance Theatre Laboratory, the O'Neill Playwrights Conference, the Williamstown Theatre Festival, and many other prestigious settings. The program focuses on helping talented young people bridge the gap from the academic theater world into the professional theater world. Past participants, scholarship recipients, and awardees have gone to work on Broadway and in London's West End, as well as in film and on television, with credits on *Bloody Bloody Andrew Jackson*, *Numbers*,

De Gustibus

Many artists no doubt consider the Kennedy Center to be our "national theater." We consider it the "Reduced Shakespeare Company Theater." The Terrace has been our semiannual home seven times (and counting) since 1994, and it's an honor and thrill to perform there. Every time we see that magnificent shoebox on the banks of the Potomac, we pinch ourselves and say, "What a glorious institution. Why the hell do they keep booking us?" There really is no accounting for taste.

—Austin Tichenor and Reed Martin

Austin Tichenor and Reed Martin are the writers and managing partners of the Reduced Shakespeare Company.

Camelot

Playwriting—any creative action—is a lonely business; I doubt there is an artist who has not wondered if there were indeed anyone out there listening, hearing, seeing. Really listening, hearing, seeing. Experiencing us through our work. Do we, did we matter? It seems that we do.

The recent Kennedy Center retrospective of my work—Terrence McNally's Nights at the Opera—is the unquestioned highlight of my career as a playwright. I have had my share of awards but this was something else entirely. It was the kind of recognition I never dared imagine.

The Center has always stood for the best in the performing arts—whether from Broadway or Mumbai or Tel Aviv or Johannesburg. It is both our national center for the performing arts and home to a fantastic panoply of artists from abroad. There is not a New Yorker who does not wish it were located some two hundred miles north, on the banks of the Hudson, rather than on the Potomac.

I have had plays premiere at the Center and have seen some of my older work in revival there. The productions have always been impeccable and the participation of

D.C. audiences—with their keen intelligence, good humor, and palpable generosity—has been one I have always welcomed. An artist is in good hands at the Kennedy Center. That is why so many of the very greatest keep coming back.

And that is in no small part because of the Center's president, Michael Kaiser, a man of great practicality and even greater vision. He makes the impossible happen against increasingly impossible odds. He knows that the arts do matter, that the world would be a poorer place without them. But he also knows they cannot be taken for granted. They must be kept fertile and relevant by generations of new artists. And they must be paid for in dollars and cents.

The Kennedy Center for the Performing Arts is our American Camelot. We must all of us take very good care of it.

—Terrence McNally

TERRENCE McNALLY is a playwright. He has written *Love! Valour! Compassion!*, *Master Class*, *Ragtime* (the musical), and *The Lisbon Traviata*.

The 39 Steps, Big Love, Lost, 24, In the Heights, Desperate Housewives, The Big Bang Theory, and *Sons of Anarchy.*

For a time the Center had a virtual theater, the Fund for American Plays, that put money toward scripts and productions staged not in the building but across the country. Like a modern-day Works Progress Administration program, the Fund meant to encourage playwrights and regional theaters and to seed new and enduring works. A few of the latter, such as *Angels in America*, *The Kentucky Cycle*, and *The Heidi Chronicles*, not only sprouted but also grew strong. The seed money paid many a salary, lighting bill, and rehearsal room charge.

New Directions and a Daring Experiment

In 1985, intent on energizing American theater, Roger Stevens hired Peter Sellars as an artistic director, with orders to establish the American National Theater. Only twenty-seven years old, Sellars brought a reputation as an *enfant terrible* that his tenure at the Center did nothing to contradict. Steering a provocative course, Sellars took theater at the Center on a detour that generated great excitement and much press. However, many area theatergoers didn't respond. The American National Theater brought adventurous souls to free performances by Mabou Mines, the Wooster Group, Dario Fo, and other outsider companies in the Terrace-level Theater Lab space, but larger and pointedly challenging productions such as *Idiot's Delight*, Sophocles'

Ajax, and a critically acclaimed *The Count of Monte Cristo* didn't draw, and subscriptions suffered. Within eighteen months, Sellars moved on, and Stevens let the national theater concept rest.

A New Era Begins

Less than two years after the departure of Peter Sellars, the Center was to see another very high-profile exit. In 1988, the Center's leader and the de facto head of all things theatrical decided to move on. Roger Stevens stepped down. At his direction, the board elected Ralph Davidson, previously chairman of TIME, Inc., to be president and chairman. It is no slight to Davidson to say that Roger Stevens was a tough act to follow, and that the top job at the Center is a huge challenge. With the staff providing momentum and managerial presence, Davidson, who never did precisely fit into the machine that Stevens had created, was able to focus on arranging a significant endowment from the government of Japan. A man from the world of communications, Davidson looked unblinkingly at systems that

Peter Sellars's daring, innovative production of Count of Monte Cristo, *based an adaptation by Peter O'Neill (Eugene's father) of the novel by Alexandre Dumas, was performed at the Kennedy Center during the 1984–1985 season.*

The Place and the People

Some theaters make you think, Oh please, not again. But the Kennedy Center feels like a home away from home. One reason is the place itself. The Eisenhower Theater is one of the most perfect spaces, visually and acoustically — precisely the right size. Another reason is the people. There's such a cast of characters. You show up and there's Max Woodward, and the same prop person and the same electrician. The Center has continuity. Like I said, home.

—Richard Thomas

RICHARD THOMAS has played the Kennedy Center many times and on many stages. He appeared on Broadway in David Mamet's *Race* and Michael Frayn's *Democracy*, starred in made-for-TV movies *The Red Badge of Courage* and *All Quiet on the Western Front*, and won an Emmy for his performance in the hit series *The Waltons*.

Richard Thomas as Edmond Dantes. In Sellars's The Count of Monte Cristo, *actors' faces were painted startling hues to indicate different aspects of their character. Critics were divided on the effect, as they were on the entire production.*

needed replacement in the aging physical plant. Expertise in systems and system reform may not be the showiest of accomplishments, but they are vital to any organization's success. Before his two years of service ended, Davidson oversaw an overhaul of the telephone systems. That task may read as minor and mundane, but it dramatically improved the efficiency of an institution that in those pre-PC days depended on phones for selling tickets, soliciting donations, answering public queries, and scheduling thousands of performances a year. Davidson's key contribution during his tenure was to formalize the organization of the Center. No small task.

Two years later, in 1990, the board elected Australian-born James Wolfensohn chairman. A banker and amateur cellist who fenced on his country's 1956 Olympic team, Wolfensohn was an energetic and ambitious arts advocate.

Wolfensohn made many significant contributions during his time as

Patti LuPone also starred in the 1985 production of The Count of Monte Cristo.

Top Left: *Kennedy Center President Lawrence J. Wilker joined the Center in 1991.*

Top Right: *Four Kennedy Center Chairmen—(from left to right) James Wolfensohn, Stephen A. Schwarzman, David M. Rubenstein (current Chairman), and James A. Johnson—pose together at a Kennedy Center event.*

chairman. He understood that unless Congress amended the 1958 law authorizing the Center, its finances would remain problematic. In addition, he saw that the Center, which under Stevens had seen the founder's personal generosity partly obscure the need for a formal fund-raising apparatus and fiscal activism among board members, needed a serious institutional means of enhancing revenue obtained through ticket sales, grants, and federal support.

To solidify the Center's finances and to manage the building more efficiently, Wolfensohn persuaded Congress to rewrite the National Cultural Center Act. In 1994, with bipartisan support, Congress authorized the transfer to the board of all appropriated fund responsibilities, thereby making one entity responsible for the physical plant and for the activities of the living presidential memorial. Direct appropriations to the Center included the creation of a capital improvements fund to cover much-needed repairs. First came a new roof and then extensive renovations to bring the building into compliance with the Americans with Disabilities Act. Based on two decades of experience staging every manner of performance, management incorporated into these efforts a thorough refitting of the theaters, from cutting cable troughs to improving acoustics to adding capacity for operating automated sets. The Concert Hall was the first to undergo renovation.

Wolfensohn also contributed greatly to the artistic identity of the Center. Convinced that the Center's president should be an entertainment professional, Wolfensohn recruited Lawrence J. (Larry) Wilker away from Cleveland's Playhouse Square Foundation. In

Matthew Broderick (left) starred as J. Pierrepont Finch with Megan Mullally (right) in How to Succeed in Business Without Really Trying *in 1995; the production moved to Broadway directly after its run at the Center.*

Tina Fey entertains the audience with her acceptance speech for the 2010 Mark Twain Prize.

Cleveland, Wilker had raised the funds for a complete renovation while at the same time putting on a stream of successful plays and musicals. At the Center, Wilker, whose tenure spanned the chairmanships of Wolfensohn and successor James A. Johnson, made resonant creative contributions and lent managerial depth as well as an important continuity to operations.

After Stevens retired, theater at the Center went through phases, sometimes emphasizing musicals, sometimes more inclined to plays. A middle era saw its meatiest stagecraft occur beneath the festival banner, as troupes from around the country and the world found the edge and balanced there. During Wilker's term, the Center dialed back in-house dramatic producing in favor of booking out-of-town tryouts for musicals. Some of Wilker's biggest successes were revivals of *Guys and Dolls*, *The King and I*, and *How to Succeed in Business Without Really Trying*. Theater still made its mark, but usually as part of festivals that were becoming increasingly large and varied, reaching to include all the art forms.

Changing of the Guard for the Silver Anniversary

With finances in clearer focus, a reenergized board swung into action, stepping up fund-raising and doing its part to see the Center through another change when Wolfensohn left in 1995 to become president of the World Bank. Trustees Alma Gildenhorn and James Evans held the fort during the search for a replacement. That exercise led to the election of James A. Johnson, who became chairman in 1996, the Center's twenty-fifth anniversary.

Under Johnson, a businessman and Democratic Party power broker, the Center continued to make improvements made possible by fiscal reorganization. Modernization of the Center's finances, governance, and physical plant was mirrored in the evolving relationship between the chairman and the CEO. Johnson relied on Wilker and the Center staff, moving further from the Stevens model to one more like those of other major arts organizations. Executive duties shifted from the chairman to the president, who effectively became the CEO.

Johnson's contributions included Performing Arts for Everyone—a menu of innovations that included broader participation in the discount Ticket Place pavilion on Seventh Street NW, the Metro shuttle, and a larger Open House. All this was undertaken in 1997 to connect the Center more fully with the city and to enhance its role as a memorial to the late president by diversifying the breadth of programming, reaching a broader audience, and making presentations available and accessible to all. The effort also led to the expansion of the parking garages at either end of the building, an undertaking completed in 2004.

Johnson and Wilker added an item to the Center calendar in 1998 that became a sensational media event: the Mark Twain Prize for American Humor. The Twain Prize goes annually to an artist who has made significant contributions to American comedy in the same vein as Twain, who applied his wit to entertain but also to illuminate, educate, and inform.

The two-night event comprises the official ceremony, taped for broadcast later, and a private dinner at which fellow comedians rib the winner. Twain Prizes have gone to Richard Pryor (1998), Jonathan Winters (1999), Carl Reiner (2000), Whoopi Goldberg (2001), Bob Newhart (2002), Lily Tomlin (2003), Lorne Michaels (2004), Steve Martin (2005), Neil Simon (2006), Billy Crystal (2007), George Carlin (2008), Bill Cosby (2009), Tina Fey (2010), and Will Ferrell (2011). At his 2005 investiture, Martin captured the spirit of the night.

"I am so proud to be here in Washington, D.C., which I have just recently learned is the nation's capital, and to receive this coveted Mark Twain Prize, which is the only significant American reward for comedy, except for money," the comic-actor-author deadpanned. "When I look at the list of people who have been given this award, it makes me very, very satisfied. But when I look at the list of people who haven't been given this award, it makes me even more satisfied."

A Festival to Usher in a New Millennium and a New President

In 2000, Larry Wilker announced his plans to give up the Center presidency. As a successor, Johnson and the board recruited Michael M. Kaiser. The new president brought a broad perspective, an ambitious agenda, and a desire to take the Kennedy Center to a new level of programming. Soon after his January 2001 arrival, Kaiser announced plans for a festival honoring composer Stephen Sondheim, an arrangement for a decade's worth of yearly appearances by the Mariinsky Opera and Ballet (formerly Kirov), and the creation of a new arts management institute, as well as an extensive plan to link the Center to the D.C. street grid (a plan that was eventually undone by a straitened federal budget).

Taking a new tack, Kaiser unfurled the entire coming season's schedule,

Pulling Together

Stage managing at the Kennedy Center is an extraordinary experience. My job is to help pull together all elements of a production, from directors to choreographers to actors to designers, starting with rehearsals and carrying through performance. The Center often collaborates with a show's creators, so the level of production is extremely high and complex. Ragtime involved more than one hundred people specific to the production, including forty-one stagehands, thirty-eight performers, and a twenty-eight-piece orchestra playing full orchestrations.

—Shari Silberglitt Moxley

SHARI SILBERGLITT MOXLEY, a contract Equity stage manager at the Center since 2002, has worked on *Sunday in the Park with George, The Glass Menagerie, Mame, Carnival!, August Wilson's 20th Century, Broadway: Three Generations, Ragtime, Master Class, Follies,* and other productions.

spurring enthusiasm among supporters, subscribers, and the press. The Institute for Arts Management at the Kennedy Center matriculated its first dozen fellows, who met for the second time the morning of September 11, 2001. Forced to close that day, the Center reopened the next and less than two weeks later presented a concert dedicated to the memory of the thousands of victims.

At that winter's Honors, the Catherine B. Reynolds Foundation Series for Artistic Excellence was announced. The first performance in the series was a rare joint appearance by the Bolshoi Opera and Ballet and Orchestra.

Stephen A. Schwarzman, elected to head the board in 2004, maintained and improved upon the balance of effort between chairman and president that has come to characterize the Center's management. Schwarzman's enthusiastic fund-raising further solidified Center finances. His personal support for theatrical productions was a shining example of generosity in action. With Schwarzman vigorously tending to the chairman's tasks, Kaiser worked across the Center's calendar, focusing on diverse, high-quality programming; expanding and focusing education offerings; and the the founding, funding, and growth of the DeVos Institute for Arts. While managing ballet and opera companies around the United States and in England, Kaiser had conceived of presenting great American writers' work by applying an innovative take on the classic repertory approach: assemble a first-rate company of performers, directors, and designers; schedule a closely spaced series of shows by the artist, with rotating productions sharing stages and people; immerse the troupe in a demanding rehearsal period; and present the result in tandem with corollary events such as symposia and concerts.

The Mariinsky Opera production of Otello *appeared at the Center in December 2007, one month after its Moscow debut. Directed by the up-and-coming 24-year-old Vasily Barkhatov and conducted by the company's General Director Valery Gergiev, it was widely praised.*

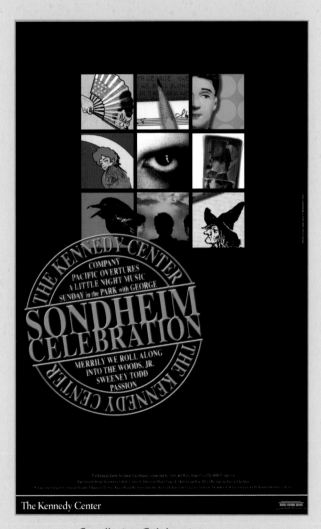

Sondheim Celebration poster

Synergy was the essence of 2002's Sondheim Celebration, a season-long festival-style examination of the composer's creativity. The lens was a series of six new productions of *Sweeney Todd, Company, Sunday in the Park with George, Merrily We Roll Along, Passion*, and *A Little Night Music*, enhanced by other presentations. One was a public conversation between Stephen Sondheim and journalist Frank Rich. That ticketed session was booked into the Terrace Theater until demand promoted it to the Concert Hall. Festival audience members came from all fifty states and thirty-eight countries.

To accompany the musicals, Barbara Cook and Mandy Patinkin performed showcases of Sondheim material. The Center presented a Japanese-language production of *Pacific Overtures* and a children-oriented version of *Into the Woods*.

Stephen Sondheim remembers, "The 2002 Festival was one of the high spots of my professional life, due to the enthusiasms of Michael Kaiser and Eric Schaeffer. I have no overview of the Center's place in American culture—I'm just glad that it's there. It would be nice if it could be the home of an American National Theater, like the Royal National Theatre in London, but Washington isn't the center of theatrical activity in this country, so I fear it can never happen. Still, as a tourist magnet, the Center helps publicize the theater in this country, and to that extent it has value above and beyond its individual presentations."

Brian Strokes Mitchell and Christine Baranski starred in the 2002 revival of Sweeney Todd.

Full Circle

When I was sixteen, my family came up from Miami for a weekend in Washington. We visited the Kennedy Center. I asked an usher if I could peek into the Opera House, which was dark.

Absolutely not, she said.

I asked again.

No way.

Disappointed, I walked back to my parents and said, "Someday I'm gonna work here."

Fifteen years later, I walked into a rehearsal room above the Opera House, ready to start work on Sondheim's Sunday in the Park with George. *That morning I'd won an Obie and been nominated for a Drama Desk Award for* tick, tick ... BOOM!. *I walked out into the Grand Foyer and burst into tears.*

Michael Kaiser's vision of staging Sondheim musicals in repertory was extraordinary—exactly what the Center should be doing: presenting the work of a great American composer, no expenses spared, for standing-room only audiences.

One day we were working on the music to "Sunday." They didn't need me, so I went for a walk. I opened the rehearsal room door, and in fell Christine Baranski, who was playing Mrs. Lovett in Sweeney Todd. She'd been listening at the door. Around the corner, Alice Ripley was practicing "Bobby, Bobby baby" from Company. In the next hall down, Brian Stokes Mitchell was singing "Joanna Part 2" from Sweeney Todd. It was a magical musical theater summer camp, there on the banks of the Potomac. We don't have a national theater in the United States, but the summer of the Sondheim Celebration that's what the Kennedy Center was.

Backstage was a labyrinth. You'd learn the codes and the secret handshakes to get around without getting lost. We used the same dressing rooms, so we'd leave one another notes. Len Cariou, the original Sweeney Todd, stopped by and wrote "Sweeney was here" on the mirror.

There was so much happening—our shows, the Opera, the Symphony, concerts in the Foyer, world leaders in the audience. It was a hive of theatrical inspiration, and the Celebration was a grand vision.

At the end of the run, I went into the empty Opera House. I walked onto the stage and said, "Here I am."

—Raúl Esparza

RAÚL ESPARZA, honored and acclaimed for performances on Broadway in works by David Mamet, Harold Pinter, Stephen Sondheim, and many others, has been nominated for Tony Awards in all four acting categories.

Left: *Raúl Esparza considers his performance in* Sunday in the Park with George *a breakout role in his career.*

Above: *Sondheim on Sondheim poster for a public interview of the celebrated composer and lyricist by Frank Rich.*

Blair Brown stars as Desiree Armfedlt in the Sondheim Celebration's 2002 production of A Little Night Music, *in which she performs one of the most famous of Sondheim's songs, "Send in the Clowns."*

Just Another Day at the Kennedy Center

While in rehearsals for Company *I found myself literally kneeling before Stephen Sondheim's oxfords (or were they loafers?). Soon after, as I experimented (some might say showed off) with the blocking for my big number, I sang "Getting Married Today" while holding a bouquet and hanging by my knees from a piece of the set. When I asked later what he thought of my antics, Steve said, simply and with his signature shy/wry smile, something like, "All you need to do is sing the words." I thought, "I can do that!"*

—Alice Ripley

ALICE RIPLEY won the 2009 Tony and Helen Hayes Best Actress Awards for her performance in the Pulitzer Prize-winning musical *Next to Normal.*

Alice Ripley performs in the 2002 revival of the 1970 musical Company, *starring as Amy, the neurotic fiancée who gets cold feet on her wedding day.*

Michael Hayden (at the piano) and the Company perform a number from the musical Merrily We Roll Along as part of the Sondheim Celebration. Raúl Esparza, Miriam Shor, and Emily Skinner also appeared in the 2002 production of the musical.

Wonderful

The people at the Center are wonderful to work with. I've never experienced anything but affection and love and helpfulness there. Michael Kaiser does wonderful work. He proved that you could take a great and challenging idea like the Sondheim festival, and do it brilliantly. Washington has become quite an arts scene, and the Center has something to do with that, as well as being very important to the arts scene nationwide.

—Barbara Cook

BARBARA COOK, namesake of the Center's Spotlight cabaret series, has earned numerous Tony, Grammy, Drama Desk, and New York Drama Critics Circle awards and nominations. During the 2002 Sondheim Celebration, she twice presented at the Center her Olivier Award-nominated show, *Barbara Cook in Mostly Sondheim.*

Barbara Cook's outstanding career stretches from her break-through role starring in the 1956 Broadway production of Candide *to acclaimed performances, especially of Sondheim songs, into her eighties. In 2011 she was named a Kennedy Center Honoree.*

There are those who believe that until you've heard Barbara Cook sing a song, you haven't heard it sung.

BARBARA COOK
a concert for the theater
Wally Harper, Musical Director

Beginning December 12   Kennedy Center Terrace Theater

Group Sales 634-7201   **INSTANT-CHARGE (202) 857-0900**   Information 254-9895

A Fall Theater Guild Subscription Attraction

Poster for the Royal Shakespeare Company's 2007 production of Shakespeare's Coriolanus *at the Center. Christine Baranski starred in the title role of the 2006 production of* Mame.

A New Theater

After thirty-five years the Center might have seemed to make maximum use of its physical plant, but it wasn't through building theaters. In 2005, the American Film Institute, which years before had moved its headquarters to Los Angeles, shut down the cinema nestled behind the Eisenhower Theater. Familiar with double-teaming the Theater Lab space between children's theater and *Shear Madness*, the staff looked at the former AFI domain and saw . . . the Family Theater, where parents and schools could bring youngsters for an introduction to theatergoing. The change was made, and since then the easily accessible Family Theater has become one of the hottest tickets in town. In addition, the Family Theater sometimes hosts more sophisticated fare, sometimes as part of Center festivals or presented by local theater companies, aimed at grown-up audiences.

In 2006, the Center produced a well-regarded revival of *Mame* and in 2009 continued in that vein with a revival of *Ragtime* that caught fire and burned a path to Broadway, as if to remind not only critics and theatergoers but also the Center itself of its profound capacity to create. Those creative powers were on full display in 2011 when the Center produced an acclaimed revival of *Follies*, starring Bernadette Peters, Danny Burstein, Jan Maxwell, Ron Raines, and Elaine Page, which moved to Broadway amid enthusiastic reviews.

As the Kennedy Center begins its fifth decade, its theatrical side occupies an enviable perch. The view backward reveals a long list of highly successful original productions and coproductions, as well as a few ambitious misses. The Center has shown an interest and respect for traditional theater, as illustrated by its relationship with the Royal Shakespeare Company, who have performed classics including *Coriolanus*, *The Taming of the Shrew*, and *Richard III*. At the same time, the Center also looks to the future, finding new talents and new productions. The future is what you make it, and prominent among what the Kennedy Center makes is great theater.

Marcia Milgrom Dodge directed the 2009 revival of Ragtime, *which made its debut at the Center prior to its move to Broadway. In D.C., Quentin Earl Darrington (left) starred as Coalhouse Walker, Jr.; Jennlee Shallow as Sarah; Darrington also appeared in the New York production.*

Michael M. Kaiser, the Center's president, is world renowned for his expertise in arts management. He is the author of several books, including The Art of the Turnaround: Creating and Maintaining Healthy Arts Organizations, *a widely read classic in its field.*

Michael M. Kaiser has the duties of chief administrator and artistic director, echoing the role Roger L. Stevens staked out. Kaiser also presides over the DeVos Institute of Arts Management at the Kennedy Center, an entity whose creation led his "to-do" list when he returned to the capital in 2001 to assume the Center presidency. He moves with ease among these three demanding assignments, less a nimble juggler than an attentive manager convinced that each reinforces the others.

Kaiser grew up in a New Rochelle, New York, family rooted in both culture and commerce. His grandfather played violin with the New York Philharmonic, while his father, a lumber wholesaler, wanted his son to be a dentist. At first keen to be an opera singer, the young Kaiser set aside that goal for a nomadic undergraduate career—four colleges in four years. He took a degree in economics at Brandeis University, then a master's degree at Massachusetts Institute of Technology's Sloan School of Management. After MIT he started and ran a successful consulting company headquartered in Washington, D.C., across the street from the Center. He wrote the books *Understanding the Competition: A Practical Guide of Competitive Analysis* and *Developing Industry Strategies: A Practical Guide of Industrial Analysis.*

A harsh epiphany propelled Kaiser out of practicing the art of business and into managing the business of the arts. In 1985, he was a six-day-a-week man, living the hard-charging executive life, when he found himself face up on the terminal floor at Detroit's Metro Airport. He'd collapsed.

"It was time to make some changes," he wrote in his 2008 book, *The Art of the Turnaround.*

Pondering which changes to make, and how to make them, Kaiser realized that while he may have given up his boyhood dream of a singing career, he still could have a life in the arts. During the summer he offered his energy and time to Washington Opera general director Martin Feinstein. Kaiser was invited to join the Opera's board.

He enjoyed that involvement, but wanted more, which meant working his way in and then up. He sold his company and began a job search, focusing on arts organizations in dire financial straits. As Kaiser observes in *Turnaround*, by its nature the arts world offers many such opportunities.

Kaiser was hired first as general manager by the Kansas City Ballet. There, he eliminated an ominous deficit while improving management and programming. In sequence he achieved similar feats as executive director of the Alvin Ailey American Dance Theater, the American Ballet Theatre (ABT), and the Royal Opera House at Covent Garden, the largest arts organization in the United Kingdom and home to the Royal Opera and Royal Ballet. At each stop along his fifteen-year journey of reinvention, Kaiser showed growing acumen at erasing deficits, improving revenues, structuring organizations, and working with staffs and boards of directors to deliver the best programming possible. While in New York with the Ailey company and the ABT, he taught as an adjunct professor in New York University's arts management master's program and wrote *Strategic Planning in the Arts: A Practical Guide*. Throughout, he was gaining confidence in his own programming sensibilities and skills. By 2000, when he was ready to leave the Royal Opera House, Kaiser knew he wanted his next job to involve the artistic side as much as finance. The Kennedy Center drew his interest for its central management structure, its cross-disciplinary possibilities, and its youth.

"Even though it's been around for forty years, the Kennedy Center is a young institution. When the Center came into being, the cultural center was a new concept in the United States and the world. Lincoln Center was dedicated in 1964 and completed in 1966; the Kennedy Center opened in 1971. There were no other such places," he said. "And as a young institution the Center is on a journey of discovery, learning its potential and trying to understand what it will be. The real challenge facing a national cultural center is to understand its possibilities. The assumption was that the Center would be bringing the arts from other places to Washington and the United States. And for forty years the Center has been experimenting with that role, sometimes succeeding, sometimes failing."

Arriving in January 2001, Kaiser was ready for the challenges of presenting good art and quality education and obtaining the money to do so. Armed with a five-year plan meant to keep activities in focus across their breadth and length, he began work on such projects as establishing an institute to educate arts managers and organizing a festival celebrating composer Stephen Sondheim. As those and other efforts got underway, however, history intervened.

The technology bubble burst, slamming investment markets and sapping charitable donations. That September al Qaeda struck; Kaiser and other Center managers were meeting with the inaugural class of Arts Institute fellows on the Terrace level when American Airlines Flight 77 hit the Pentagon. Within weeks the capital was besieged by sniper attacks that kept many area residents home. An anthrax scare snarled the mail.

But the Center pressed on, gradually regaining momentum. Kaiser directed an appraisal and reorganization of education programs, streamlining offerings, focusing on the most potent elements, and developing powerful new programs such as Any Given Child, aimed at providing equity and access to arts education by combining the resources of the school district, local arts groups, and the Center. The program, designed for students in grades K–8 is now in seven cities and about to be expanded.

To restore emphasis and programming that had languished, dance and ballet underwent a rebuilding that included the creation of the Ballet Across America and Protégés events, and the creation of the Conservatory Project. National Symphony Orchestra funding rose to support more touring and guest artist appearances. The Sondheim Celebration was a resounding success, followed by similarly resonant treatments of playwrights Tennessee Williams and August Wilson .

Convinced that Center festivals could clear a higher bar, Kaiser called a hiatus to rethink and refresh the approach. The tradition reemerged winningly with the Festival of China and has continued with celebrations of Japan, the Arab world, jazz, and, in 2011, India.

"Every year we hope to keep bringing programming that some people might say doesn't belong at the Center, such as our Country Music Festival, the A Cappella Festival, and the Gospel Music Festival. I want to expand the institution's bandwidth," Kaiser said. "It's important to note that the festivals didn't begin with me, but began much earlier. What I was able to do was to think through what the festivals could accomplish by taking advantage of the potential cross-disciplinary interactions that are implicit at the Center. The India festival that took place last [2011] season is

a good example. These festivals grow out of our history and they are being honored in the traditional way by being copied by other arts organizations, like Carnegie Hall."

Festivals present the Center as the broad and diverse institution it truly is, a corrective to the typecasting that can result from such immensely popular events as the Kennedy Center Honors and the Mark Twain Prize. The planning behind festivals is as intense as that accorded other endeavors at the Center, whose view must be as broad as possible yet strive never to let the details slip.

"Artistic planning involves so many forms, and you have to spotlight all those forms," Kaiser said. "At a smaller arts organization, it's possible, even inevitable, to specialize. You put on six productions a year, so you necessarily have to focus on them and on the base audience and supporters of your organization. At the Center, we can't do that. Our mandate is to serve everyone. You have to manage very carefully. The president of the Kennedy Center can't favor one form over another. You have to focus on all art forms. That's why it's so useful to have five-year artistic plans. You can look five years out and see whether the plan is balanced and whether you are playing favorites."

The Center is superb at presenting dance and ballet, at arts management training, and at international undertakings, which, according to Kaiser, serve the U.S. State Department as a cultural ambassador. "We are very strong at tying together art forms," he said. "That is something that is special that the Center does."

During his final years as Center president, Kaiser will be looking forward to teaching and traveling more, but he won't be pondering his next assignment; he's already on the job. "I'm going to be president of the Kennedy Center for four more years, and I'm president of the DeVos Institute now. When I leave the Center I'll be devoting myself full-time to the Institute, but I'm not waiting to do things at the Institute," he said. "I'm taking action now. We have training programs in seven cities and an international presence, as well as arrangements with a major university. On the international side, the goal is to create and build a cadre of trained managers who will return to their countries and teach arts management. In the United States, we want to build a very strong pool of people to run arts organizations and serve as arts organization board members. We are developing online programs that enable all these people to get in touch and stay in touch with one another."

In writing about and teaching the intricacies of managing arts organizations, Kaiser advocates a "family" model that works non-stop to emphasize performance quality and increase audience participation and financial support.

"The family model that I embrace for arts organizations is in good shape at the Kennedy Center. It's a terrific way to add new members and new supporters, and we have done a good job on the family approach here," he says. "Our funding is strong. It was less than $35 million and now it's $75 million. We have more donors, and more big donors. The last ten years the Center has had an annual surplus, even in bad times. Our ticket buyers, our subscribers, our board, and our donors—all constituencies are happy. Of course, no family is always happy all the time. The Center continues to evolve. In four years, I'll leave and someone else will take this job and do things differently, which is as it should be. Even after forty years it's not necessarily so that an institution like this has figured itself out. It's a different place every five years, and that's exciting to see."

Legacy

Growing up in Detroit, I experienced my first sense of global awareness in the aftermath of President Kennedy's assassination. The Kennedy family embodies a deep sense of pride in culture and in the arts that profoundly affects me to this day. Working at the Center, the American pinnacle of music, art, and theater, I felt an overwhelming responsibility to live up to that legacy of excellence, to strengthen my craft, and to do my best work. I will forever be grateful to the Center's President, Michael Kaiser, for giving me that opportunity and for calling me an artist.

—Marcia Milgrom Dodge

MARCIA MILGROM DODGE directed and choreographed the Center's 2009 production of *Ragtime*, which won four Helen Hayes Awards, including Outstanding Direction, Resident Musical. *Ragtime* transferred to Broadway and received seven Tony Award nominations, including Best Director of a Musical, and nine Drama Desk Award nominations. Dodge is the first woman to direct and choreograph a major musical produced by the Center.

TENNESSEE WILLIAMS EXPLORED

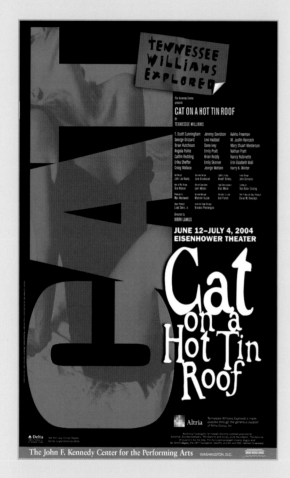

Mary Stuart Masterson and Jeremy Davidson star in a steamy scene from Cat on a Hot Tin Roof *during the Tennessee Williams Explored Festival.*

In 2004, the Center celebrated Tennessee Williams. The festival presented new productions of *A Streetcar Named Desire*, *Cat on a Hot Tin Roof*, and *The Glass Menagerie*, starring Patricia Clarkson, George Grizzard, and Sally Field. The festival also included a symposium of leading actresses Rosemary Harris, Estelle Parsons, Zoe Caldwell, and Eva Marie Saint discussing characters they'd played, their relationships with the playwright, and the shows themselves.

Sally Field starred as Amanda Wingfield, mother of the crippled Laura in the Glass Menagerie, directed by Gregory Mosher. The play was the third of three Williams classics performed during Tennessee Williams Explored and received rave reviews.

Soul

I love the Kennedy Center, and I love how much it's used—as a theater should be. It's one of those places that were part of the circuit. You'd see someone on the road and ask, "What's up, then?" and they'd say, "Oh, I'm at the Kennedy Center for four weeks, and then I play Philadelphia for two and half." It was an element of the routine, part of the year as you were earning your living. I feel as if I grew up in American theater at the Center. I know the stagehands and the dressers and the people who take care of the wigs, the soul of the place. When I'd get there the first thing I'd do was go around and say, "Hello, how's your mum, and how's your sister, and how are you?"

—Zoe Caldwell

ZOE CALDWELL has won four Tony Awards for performances on Broadway in Tennessee Williams's *Slapstick Tragedy, The Prime of Miss Jean Brodie, Medea,* and *Master Class.* Her Kennedy Center appearances include those plays and many others, including *Long Day's Journey into Night, Medea, Master Class,* and *Lillian.*

Zoe Caldwell discussed her work in Tennessee Williams's plays at a symposium during the Williams festival. Here, she stars as Lillian, written by William Luce, based on the life of Lillian Hellman (author of The Little Foxes*).*

Like Gold

I adore the Kennedy Center.

I grew up in Richmond, Virginia, and as a child was taken to many productions there. I saw amazing national tours—Medea with Judith Anderson and Zoe Caldwell, the list is vast. I'm convinced that witnessing such vibrant, masterfully done theater at such a young age is why I do what I do today.

When you're performing at the Center, you're made to feel like a treasured guest. The staff treats you like gold, with love, care, enthusiasm, and respect. And as a producing entity, the Center operates with a sense of mission and a fantastic energy. Having performed in four shows there over the past decade, I think I can honestly say that they are my favorite producers to work for. The Center encourages its artists to go full force. They bring every resource at their disposal to bear on every single production. It's the best possible way to produce, and I'm certain it is a primary reason why artists around the world clamor to appear there. They don't do anything by half-measures, the taste quality is superb, and everything is done with a full heart. They clearly understand that great theater connects us all to our humanity and that therefore theater has an important job to do. Did I mention that I love the Kennedy Center?

—Emily Skinner

EMILY SKINNER appeared at the Center in the Sondheim Celebration productions of *Company* and *Merrily We Roll Along*, as well as in *Cat on a Hot Tin Roof* and *Mame*.

Zoe Caldwell (left) won a Tony Award for her role as Medea while costar Judith Anderson (right) received a nomination as the Nurse in the 1983 version of the Greek tragedy.

AUGUST WILSON'S 20TH CENTURY

In 2008, August Wilson's 20th Century brought fully staged readings of the late playwright's *Pittsburgh Cycle* to the Center. Ten gripping plays whose settings span a hundred years but whose subject is timeless. Wilson was an alchemist, applying a combination of talent, wit, and relentless work to the theme of being black in America. In a brief, busy life (he died in 2005, at sixty), Wilson transmuted pain into treasure with work that earned him tremendous honors, including two Pulitzer Prizes and an Emmy.

The playwright spent a quarter-century building his epic. Set mostly in Pittsburgh's Hill District, where Wilson spent his childhood, these ten plays—*Gem of the Ocean*, *The Piano Lesson*, *Two Trains Running*, *Radio Golf*, *Joe Turner's Come and Gone*, *Seven Guitars*, *Jitney*, *Ma Rainey's Black Bottom*, *Fences*, and *King Hedley II*—travel decade by decade from 1904 to 1997, conveying the African-American experience from the Middle Passage to the modern day.

To heighten the impact, the Center's readings of the Cycle plays were staged in chronological order. For five weeks, Wilson's masterworks swept up the company as Artistic Director Kenny Leon and fellow directors Lou Bellamy, Gordon Davidson, Israel Hicks, Todd Kreidler, Derrick Sanders, and Ruben Santiago-Hudson led forty-two actors through the playwright's decades. Many of them had worked with Wilson, were reading roles he'd created that they'd played elsewhere, or were appearing in several of the Center presentations. This cross-fertilization gave the series an energy that made it seem as if Wilson himself was present, and the production drew reams of praise.

This innovative strategy of clustering a group of productions with related events resonated across the country and around the world. Arts centers in many locales are adapting the Center's repertory festival model to their programming—a true testament to the Center's quality and influence. Similar programming coups are on tap in the Center's schedule for the coming years.

Harry Lennix stars as Harmond Wilks in August Wilson's 20th Century's performance of Radio Golf.

Giving Back

I never thought August Wilson would die. I felt he was the most important artist on American soil. He gave so many African-American artists opportunities to further their skills. He let us see that theater wasn't just dressing up and putting on a fur coat and stepping out. He let poor people and black people feel the power of theater. I thought he'd live forever.

But August did die. One of the highs of my career was to engage with him on his last two shows on Broadway, as he was dealing with cancer. Near the end, we were sitting on his porch in Seattle talking about life, and about being black artists, and about him finishing up those ten plays. I'll never forget those talks.

As he was passing I thought, I can't bring August back to life, but what can I do to keep him alive? One thing was the August Wilson Monologue Competition, which is held in six states and brings the three finalists to the August Wilson Theater in New York to meet mentors like Denzel Washington.

The other thing was August Wilson's 20th Century. That was one of the most important cultural events ever, with forty-two actors, seven directors, four designers, and three stage managers at our national theater holding up the work of the most important writer of the last twenty-fives years. As artists, we were giving back to August and to the country. That could have happened only at the Kennedy Center. No one had ever done all ten plays that way.

—Kenny Leon

KENNY LEON, Artistic Director of True Colors Theatre Company, was nominated for a Tony for his direction of a 2010 Broadway production of August Wilson's *Fences*. As Artistic Director for August Wilson's 20th Century, he oversaw the project and directed *Gem of the Ocean*, *Fences*, *Radio Golf*, and *The Piano Lesson*.

Ebony Jo-Ann stars as Ma Rainey in the title role of Ma Rainey's Black Bottom.

Tracie Thoms (left), as Black Mary, and Michele Shay (right), as Aunt Ester, perform in the production of Gem of the Ocean *from August Wilson's 20th Century.*

Russell Hornsby, John Beasley, Dominique Ross, LaTanya Richardson Jackson, Cherise Boothe, Michole Briana White, and Montae Russell are onstage together in a charged moment in Joe Turner's Come and Gone.

Angel Corella and Xiomara Reyes appear in the American Ballet Theatre (ABT) production of Romeo and Juliet, *2006. The ABT's long and fruitful association with the Center began when the Center opened. ABT was the official ballet company of the Center for a decade and presented the very first ballet performances at the Center in September 1971.*

II. THE DANCE BEGINS

Dance is one of the many art forms that can appeal to an audience on an almost universal level. You don't need to know the language of the performers in order to enjoy the dance. You don't require a degree in mathematics to understand the grace of the motions, the rhythm of two performers moving together. You don't even need to hear the music to feel the thrill of seeing a dancer defy gravity, fly into the air, and transform movement into a language all its own.

From the evening of the 1971 dedication, when ovations greeted Judith Jamison's performance of Bernstein's *Mass* choreographed by Alvin Ailey, to the latest works underwritten by the Local Dance Commission Program, the Center has emphasized dance. Throughout its history, the Center has developed and enjoyed enduring relationships with America's leading companies. The pride of New York City's Lincoln Center, the American Ballet Theatre and the New York City Ballet, with their classical European and American repertoires, as well as the Paul Taylor Dance Company, the Alvin Ailey American Dance Theater, Dance Theatre of Harlem, and other founders of American contemporary dance, as well as a lengthening list of city and regional companies from around the United States have made the Center a prime stop.

The Center embraced innovative dance from its first decade. Above: *A young Mikhail Baryshnikov appears in the 1976 production of Twyla Tharp's* Push Comes to Shove.

Deborah Colker

Companhia de Dança

Mix

Companhia
de Dança
Deborah Colker

October 28–30, 2010
Eisenhower Theater

The Kennedy Center

Above: *Deborah Colker's Companhia de Dança brought Brazillan energy to the Center's stage.*

Left: *Marcia Haydee and Richard Cragun dance in the Stuttgart Ballet's 1973 production of* Romeo and Juliet.

In addition to elite dance companies across the United States, the Center has also attracted the finest dancers from around the world. Whether hosting giants of European classicism such as the Bolshoi Ballet and the Royal Danish Ballet or freewheeling upstarts such as Companhia de Dança, the brainchild of Brazilian wizard Deborah Colker, the Center has seen them all. The Center has also seen performances by the Stuttgart Ballet and the Royal Ballet, the Mariinsky Ballet, the Paris Opera Ballet, and Berlin Opera Ballet, the London Festival Ballet, and the Pennsylvania Ballet. Executive Director Martin Feinstein brought in the world-famous Margot Fonteyn and Rudolf Nureyev, Natalia Makarova, Erik Bruhn, and Anthony Dowell, as well as the first of several Washington appearances by Alicia Alonso's Ballet Nacional de Cuba.

The Center has commissioned many works and produced numerous dance tours. As *Washington Post* dance critic Sara Kaufman wrote, the Kennedy Center "provided a place for dance to happen in this city like no other before or since."

Alicia Alonso performs Giselle *with Ballet Nacional de Cuba in 1978 at the Center. It was her first U.S. appearance.*

Thanks to Martin Feinstein's astute booking, rich Rolodex, and embracing personality, the Center boasted dance highlights from the start, especially in the field of ballet. The outgoing Feinstein and the low-key George Balanchine might have seemed an odd pairing, but the results of their collaboration speak for themselves. Balanchine's New York City Ballet became one of the pillars of the Center's season, along with American Ballet Theatre, which has appeared at the Center during every one of the last forty years.

Rudolf Nureyev with Nadia Potts. Rudolf Nureyev choreographed The Sleeping Beauty *for the National Ballet of Canada in 1972.*

Expanding Dance

During the 1980s, under Artistic Director Marta Istomin, the Center's dance schedule expanded to include not only more companies from abroad but also rising companies from around the United States. A comprehensive view of dance at the Center developed, as festivals presented dance in varied contexts, and offerings ventured beyond ballet and modern into folk, tap, and jazz.

That decade, the Dance America series began, sponsored jointly by the Center and the Washington Performing Arts Society. Modern dance ensembles performing as part of Dance America included Liz Lerman's Dance Exchange, Anna Sokolow's Players' Project, the Martha Graham Dance Company, and the dance companies of Paul Taylor, who performed *Mercuric Tidings* and *Lost, Found and Lost*, and Merce Cunningham.

The roll call of American companies appearing there lengthened. From New York came the Eliot Feld Ballet. A new *Nutcracker* by the Chicago-based Joffrey Ballet re-cast that favorite in Victorian America. The Houston Ballet visited multiple times, as did the San Francisco Ballet, and the Center's San Francisco Festival included that city's own Ethnic Dance Festival, along with the West Coast–based Oberlin Dance Company. The showcase event "Washington, Front and Center!" brought nine local metropolitan area dance organizations to perform at the Center.

Dance programs also showed a great deal of international influence during the 1980s. While many people might associate ballet most immediately with France and Russia, the discipline has been embraced around the world. The next great ballet dancer might be from Iceland, or São Paulo, or Pretoria, and the Center has featured companies from many continents.

Mazowsze brought folkloric songs and dances from Poland, and Rudolf Nureyev and the Zurich Ballet presented *Manfred*. Ballet West, of Salt Lake City

Erica Lynette Edwards performs the Spanish Dance "Chocolate" in The Joffrey Ballet's 2006 The Nutcracker *production.*

Bonnie Pickard and Michael Cook dance in the 2008 Suzanne Farrell Ballet production of Stars and Stripes, with choreography by George Balanchine.

not only staged *Swan Lake* but also presented Danish choreographer August Bournonville's *Abdallah* in its East Coast premiere in 1985, the first time that ballet had been staged since 1855. Roland Petit's Ballet National de Marseille performed *Notre Dame de Paris*. The Royal Danish Ballet danced *Napoli*, set in Italy. The Royal Spanish National Ballet made its Washington debut, combining ballet and flamenco.

Leningrad's Mariinsky Ballet debuted at the Center with four programs, including newly acquired works by George Balanchine. The London Festival Ballet (now the English National Ballet) brought full productions of *La Sylphide* and Sir Frederick Ashton's rarely staged *Romeo and Juliet*.

American Ballet Theatre poster and insert for The Nutcracker in 1976

Heart and Soul

I was so incredibly proud and honored to bring my company to the Kennedy Center each of the four times we performed there. Dancing on that stage was a seminal moment in our young dancers' lives, one they will never forget. The invitation to perform in the symbolic home of American culture acknowledged that they represented the highest standards of artistic excellence. To me, the Center represents the cultural heart and soul of America. It is America's hugely vibrant center for the performing arts, where the best and the brightest in American and international performing arts, in all of its wondrous diversity, is welcomed and showcased.

—Edward Villella

EDWARD VILLELLA, founding Artistic Director and Chief Executive Officer of Miami City Ballet, is a holder of the National Medal of Arts and a Kennedy Center Honoree. As a Principal Dancer with the New York City Ballet, he danced for President Kennedy's inauguration.

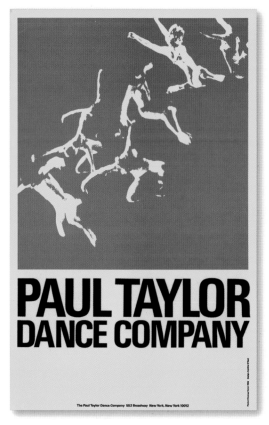

Paul Taylor Dance Company poster

Dancing Into a New Decade

During the 1990s dance received somewhat less emphasis at the Center, though the schedule still often included the form. Highlights ranged from the American Ballet Theatre's fiftieth anniversary to breakthrough modern works performed by Mark Morris's Monnaie Dance Group. The Australian Ballet and Royal Ballet of London returned, each after an absence of more than a decade. In 1993, the Center and Dance Theatre of Harlem collaborated to start a Community Initiative in Dance aimed at introducing D.C. schoolchildren to classical ballet. The France Danse Festival reflected two hundred years of French dance, from classical ballet by the Ballet de l'Opéra de Paris and Ballet du Rhin to contemporary works by Plaisir D'Offrir, Compagnie Mathilde Monnier, Compagnie Angelin Preljocaj, and Compagnie Bagouet.

The Center began a project supporting the creation of six new ballets for companies around the United States, each to have a world premiere at the Center. One of the most successful results was Paul Taylor's *Company B* with the Houston Ballet. This piece used the music and songs of the Andrews Sisters to examine America in the 1940s, a turbulent time when the country was transitioning from the Depression to World War II. Other fruits of the commissioning project included San Francisco Ballet's production of Donald McKayle's *Gumbo Ya-Ya* and the Boston Ballet's production of Merce Cunningham's *Breakers*. Another premiere, the Royal Ballet's

Magic

On those beautiful stages, it was always so easy to stay in the air on a balletic leap. It must have been that Kennedy magic.

—Jacques d'Amboise

JACQUES D'AMBOISE, a former principal dancer with the New York City Ballet, choreographer, and Kennedy Center Honoree, founded and runs the National Dance Institute.

The Houston Ballet performs the Kennedy Center–commissioned world premiere of Company B, choreographed by Paul Taylor in 1991.

Above: *Dance Theatre of Harlem poster*

Right: *A young Dance Theatre of Harlem soloist*

The Dance Theatre of Harlem performs Banda, *choreographed by Geoffrey Holder, on a 1990 visit to the Center. The Dance Theatre of Harlem has enjoyed a long, multifaceted association with the Center, presenting numerous productions and, since 1992, conducting the yearly Dance Theatre of Harlem Residency program, training young dancers from the surrounding area.*

The Royal Ballet presented a lavish production of Sleeping Beauty *in 1994.*

Sleeping Beauty, by Anthony Dowell, coincided with a gala whose guests included President and Mrs. Bill Clinton as well as Princess Margaret. Twyla Tharp's 1994 summer residency resulted in works in progress presented as *Twyla Tharp in Washington: New Works*.

Mid-decade, dance was flourishing at the Center. In 1995, the Australian Ballet introduced three dances by choreographers from down under. American Ballet Theatre danced world premieres of works by Twyla Tharp and Lar Lubovitch. The Ballet Nacional de Marseilles' Roland Petit appeared as part of Dance America, performing the new work *Chaplin Dances*.

America Dancing, a five-year retrospective on modern dance, began in 1995 with tributes to Isadora Duncan, Doris Humphrey and Thomas Weidman, and José Limón. Suzanne Farrell staged seven Balanchine masterworks, a Kennedy Center production that drew

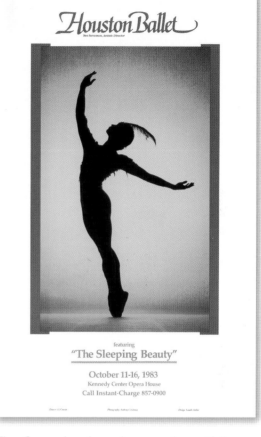

featuring
"The Sleeping Beauty"

October 11-16, 1983
Kennedy Center Opera House
Call Instant-Charge 857-0900

The Center has been home to beautifully varied productions of the classics over the years. The Houston Ballet's poster for its Sleeping Beauty *hints that their production will look quite different from that of the Royal Ballet.*

Coming Home

A great culture needs a great national center for the performing arts. The Kennedy Center is that, as well as a living monument to an inspirational leader. President Kennedy knew that one way in which future generations will take our measure is through the art we leave behind—the kind of art the Center presents day after day. It's always gratifying to have my company perform here. This community, which has followed my work from my early days, really knows dance. Its enthusiasm makes a Kennedy Center engagement one of my dancers' favorites; for me, it means coming home.

—Paul Taylor

PAUL TAYLOR, a choreographer and recipient of the National Medal for the Arts and the Kennedy Center Honors, founded the company that bears his name. He danced in the companies of George Balanchine, Merce Cunningham, and Martha Graham.

Pepito's Story dancers rehearse. Commissioned by the Center and performed in the more intimate Terrace Theater, the work features choreography by Debbie Allen and a score flavored with Caribbean rhythms and accents created by jazz superstar Arturo Sandoval.

international attention. The Martha Graham Dance Company presented a fiftieth anniversary *Appalachian Spring* and the world premiere of Robert Wilson's *Snow on the Mesa*. Choreographer Debbie Allen directed *Pepito's Story*, a dance-rich musical scored by trumpeter Arturo Sandoval and narrated by Hinton Battle.

A Move to Modernity

Dance at the Center isn't confined to ballet. In addition to offering a home for classical dance, the Center has also helped to showcase and develop new forms of modern dance, proving that dance isn't a moving museum piece but a constantly changing and evolving art form.

The Martha Graham Dance Company performs Acts of Light *in 1981.*

The work of the Bill T. Jones/Artie Zane Dance Company was part of the Center's five-year America Dancing program, celebrating the breadth and achievement of U.S.-based dance.

In 1996, Charles Reinhart and Stephanie Reinhart, codirectors of the Durham, NC–based American Dance Festival (ADF), began programming modern dance at the Center. The Reinharts carried through with America Dancing and brought new focus to the Center's modern dance schedule. Performances moved from the Terrace Theater to the Eisenhower Theater, enlarging access and increasing the audience. For one project, the Center and ADF paired noted jazz composers with selected choreographers to create new dance pieces. Over several years, a series honored modern dance work by George Balanchine, Jerome Robbins, Antony Tudor, and Sir Frederick Ashton. Another program celebrated the solo as the foundation of modern dance, from old to new.

As the decade moved toward the millennium, America Dancing showcased the work of Martha Graham and Bill T. Jones. The decade saw dance range from the very traditional to the international, such as the U.S. debut of Brazilian dancer, musician, and comedian Antonio Nóbrega.

Familiar Faces at the Close of a Millennium

During 1999–2000, the Center produced a successful U.S. tour by the Bolshoi Ballet that included a stop at the Opera House. American Ballet Theatre not only debuted a new *Swan Lake* by artistic director Kevin McKenzie but also Twyla Tharp's *Variations on a Theme* by Haydn.

The season ended with the Balanchine Celebration, a two-week homage. Appearing as part of a tour coproduced by the Center, members of the Bolshoi Ballet, including Nina Ananiashvili, Dimitri Belogolovtsev, and Sergei Filin, opened the celebration. The San Francisco Ballet rounded out the celebration with the Japanese-inflected *Bugaku*, the 1940s-era *Symphony in C*, sassy 1972 work *Symphony in Three Movements*, and 1929 classic *Prodigal Son*.

The Bolshoi Ballet's U. S. appearances during the Soviet era were mainly due to the efforts of legendary impresario Sol Hurok, who worked closely with Center chairman Roger Stevens. After a decade-long absence from the United States, their triumphant return in 2000, on a tour produced by the Center, made headlines.

Responsibility

I've always thought of the Center as my second home, after the Metropolitan Opera House in New York, and I've always felt a special connection with Washington audiences. I fondly remember dancing Swan Lake at the Center, a performance documented on the DVD I see in so many libraries. The Center is one of the world's leading stages not only because of the artists who appear there but also because of all the Center does behind the curtain. It's a model institution that has taken the performing arts to a global scale and has done so with a personal sense of responsibility to protect and support performers.

—Angel Corella

ANGEL CORELLA, Artistic Director and Principal Dancer of Corella Ballet as well as Principal Dancer with American Ballet Theatre, is a recipient of the Prix Benois de la Danse and the National Award of Spain.

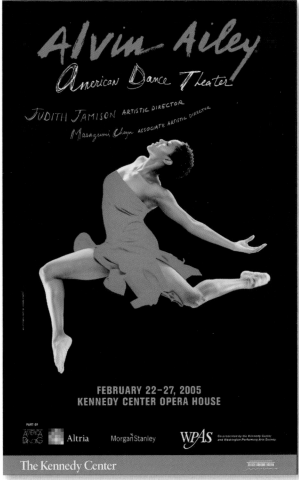

Above: *The Alvin Ailey American Dance Theater makes hugely popular annual appearances at the Center.*

Left: *Alvin Ailey American Dance Theater performs* Revelations *during the Millennium Stage 10th Anniversary in 2007.*

It was a season of classical work and innovative new ideas. The Center showcased the talents of some of the premiere names in dance. Whether it was ballet or modern dance, the decade of the nineties gave a fascinating view of where dance had come from and the possible directions it might take.

Reinvigorating Dance

Dance isn't merely about movement and rhythm. It can also be a way to communicate ideas, philosophies, and lessons. Dance can be an art form that teaches, that critiques, that challenges the audience and shatters assumptions. As calendars shifted to a new millennium, dance at the Center witnessed a great deal of daring and provocative expression.

In the first decade of the twenty-first century, dance programming at the Center regained momentum. Among

other advances, the Center welcomed The Suzanne Farrell Ballet company. Begun by its illustrious namesake, who starred often at the Center before retiring from the stage, this exuberantly talented and ambitious young company germinated as part of the Center's educational mission.

In addition to the annual appearance

of the Alvin Ailey American Dance Theater, the modern dance schedule included tap dancer Savion Glover performing with the McCoy Tyner Trio. As part of its residency, Shen Wei Dance Arts danced *Connect Transfer*, in which dancers work on a white canvas floor, hands and bodies coated with wet paint, to create a visual record of their

The Ballet Folklórico de la Universidad Veracruzana dancers brought their spectacular color and choreography to the Center's 2010 Celebrate Mexico Festival.

The Suzanne Farrell Ballet company has been in residence at the Center since 2001, but Farrell's association with the Center dates back to the 1970s.

As myriad memories, articles, books, blog posts, and online video clips attest, ballet has carried Suzanne Farrell far—a journey that has brought her again and again to the Kennedy Center. In her dancing days, she performed almost annually at the Center with the New York City Ballet from 1976 until 1983. Now she's artistic director of a company that bears her name and has been part of the Center since 2001. She still can tap into the excitement her performances delivered.

"It was wonderful to come to the nation's capital and perform here," Farrell said. "We usually came down for two weeks. I'd bring my cat, Bottom. It became like a second home." In addition to company performances, Farrell performed George Balanchine's *Tschaikovsky Pas de Deux* at the Opera House for the first Kennedy Center Honors saluting her mentor, along with other Honorees Fred Astaire, Richard Rodgers, Arthur Rubinstein, and Marian Anderson.

In 1982, while at the Center with his company, Balanchine had to be hospitalized. That episode, which deeply unsettled Farrell, began a decline that ended with the choreographer's death the next year. Balanchine left his muse several ballets he had created for her—*Meditation, Tzigane,* and *Don Quixote*—and which she performed until retiring from the stage in 1989. For several years, besides staging those bequests and other Balanchine works administered by the Balanchine Trust, Farrell ran a summer program in the Adirondacks that she had founded.

In 1993, James Wolfensohn invited Farrell to consider a project at the Center: a weekend workshop for young dancers from the Washington area. There would be no tuition. Farrell agreed. The January 1994 event was a success, and led to a two-weekend session the next year.

Interest in Farrell's own summer program soared, but it already was at capacity. The result was Exploring Ballet with Suzanne Farrell, a Center-sponsored workshop for youngsters wanting careers in dance. Word of mouth and nationwide auditions filled the first two-week session, held the summer of 1995. The Center's education department helped promising prospects with tuition. Recalling her beginnings with Balanchine, Farrell refined an instructional template.

"I tell young dancers, you're bound to spend more time in the classroom than on stage. Class is a combination of performance and a laboratory. You can learn from mistakes. It's also where you get to know one another, whether as dancer to dancer or choreographer to dancer," Farrell said. "There's interdependence; you have to know a person's strengths and weaknesses to choreograph for that person. And you always want to engage the audience. If there are a thousand people in the audience, you have to dance a thousand different ways."

The next year two young dancers from France wrote requesting admission, and the summer session went international. Within a few years Farrell was traveling worldwide—Mexico, China, and Japan, to name a few destinations—to audition candidates. Each audition amounted to a two-hour workshop with Farrell at no charge.

Eric Ragan (left) and Momchil Mladenov (right), in the title role, in The Suzanne Farrell Ballet 2005 *world premiere staging of* Balanchine's Don Quixote.

In 1996, as part of the Center's twenty-fifth anniversary celebration, Farrell presented a week of Balanchine performances. In 1999, the education department proposed a series of dance programs and tours. Farrell agreed to the undertaking, budgeted for eight to ten dancers, and had an intriguing notion.

"I could see that if I had the same dancers to work with we could develop into a company," she said. "I didn't know if I wanted to head a company. But I realized that when I was a young dancer someone had nurtured me, and provided what I needed to focus on my dancing. I couldn't have become what I did if I'd have to work as a waitress, or if there were no Lincoln Kirstein, or a theater to dance in for Mr. B. We've lost the culture of the impresario, which is a role that's different from arts management. You have to get the money, because if there's no money there's no organization."

Farrell decided to start a company of her own. In 2001, she mounted a weeklong series of performances by The Suzanne Farrell Ballet at the Center. "We're often compared to companies that have been in existence for seventy-five or a hundred years and have much larger budgets," Farrell said. "Each year has been different—ten years in the life of a dance company is not all that long a period of time."

Farrell's association with Balanchine left her with a sense of history—as well as an historic trove of dances that her company performs, in addition to pieces by Jerome Robbins and Maurice Béjart, with whom Farrell also worked. The company also devotes energy to the Balanchine Preservation Initiative, which is dedicated to performing those compositions of Balanchine's that are on the verge of extinction. "Quite a few of Mr. B's dances have been 'lost,'" Farrell said. "When you're a young dancer you don't think you'll ever grow old, or that ballets will fade away, but you do, and they do. In a sense, working with the ballet here has been a way to have a Balanchine renaissance."

With the Balanchine Trust's assent, Farrell, a repetiteur of that organization, is engaging in what might be termed artistic archaeology. Using primitive 1970s-era videotape of vintage Balanchine performances and works in progress, the Balanchine Preservation Initiative is recreating dances unseen in decades, painstakingly matching footage to the music that accompanied the movements documented to provide a guide to performing them anew. One piece, 1968's *Pithoprakta*, was taped in its entirety, offering a view of Balanchine's work in action—with one big difference.

"Eleven dancers, including Arthur Mitchell and I, danced that," Farrell said. "But when the video was shot Arthur couldn't be there. I danced alone, and you can see in the video where there should be a pas de deux. I asked the Trust if we could redo it, and they were happy to see that happen. I wondered whether the company should do it as archived or with a man, and the Trust said they wanted a man in the Mitchell role. I choreographed it."

Farrell likens the fragmentary video record to discovering King Tut's tomb. "When you come upon a piece in this fashion, such as with *Pithoprakta*, you're seeing it in the theater as the audience did, and you should feel changed," she said.

The 2005 Kennedy Center honoree is eager to keep her dancers on their toes. "We want to give the Center the best that we can do," Farrell said.

Company operations remain lean and mean, but not quite as much as at the beginning. "When we started, I was on my own. I did it all," Farrell said. "Now I have a staff. We also have the Kennedy Center Opera House Orchestra to perform with, when many companies are performing to CD. This little engine that could of ours is going uphill."

Farrell welcomes juggling the welter of details, from sets to costumes to music, that her role entails. "You become very creative. You have to be emotionally flexible and strong. The more you give, the more you have to give," she said.

Running a company has brought her a different point of view, Farrell said. "When I was performing, I looked at dance through special eyes, different eyes, than I use as a director," she said. "As a dancer I was looking out through my eyes. When I was seventeen dancing *Apollo*, I would see Apollo and two muses. But the first time I staged *Apollo* I was looking at four people. To preserve a ballet's integrity, a director has to know how to see."

Natalia Magnicaballi pauses en pointe in The Suzanne Farrell Ballet 2007 production of Bugaku, a Balanchine ballet.

movements. From New Zealand, the all-male company Black Grace, mainly made up of Pacific Islanders and Maori, melded traditional and contemporary forms.

The modern dance calendar featured Pilobolus Dance Theatre in a program of well-known and new work, including *Redline, Darkness and Light, Gnomen, Walkyndon,* and *Rushes.* Keigwin + Company performed *Elements (Water,* *Fire, Earth, and Air).* Cloud Gate Dance Theatre of Taiwan danced the full-length *Moon Water.* Resident company Shen Wei Dance Arts brought back *Re-.* From Spain, Compañia Nacional de Danza made its Washington debut dancing *Bach: Multiplicity, Forms of Silence and Emptiness,* inspired by the composer's music and life.

The Center also sought out prized local talent, in addition to companies with national reputations. To foster new works by Washington-area artists, the Center began the Millennium Stage Local Dance Commissioning Project. Commissioned works debut on Millennium Stage and are webcast live and archived digitally. Each year, commissions go to a select group of choreographers from the District of Columbia, Maryland, and Virginia, providing funds for each to create a new piece and a venue in which to premiere the work, as well as rehearsal space and technical assistance. In addition to its Millennium Stage premiere, each dance gets a showing at Dance Place in Washington, D.C.

In addition to programs focused specifically on dance, the Center also showcased dance as a key component of more diverse festivals. The more encyclopedic the Center's festivals have become, the more dance they have incorporated, a mark of the art form's significance in culture and national identity. Sometimes a festival consists entirely of dance, as in 2005's Masters of African American Choreography, which honored the profound influence on

Special

The Center is very special for me because it is in one of the first cities I performed in as a member of American Ballet Theatre. My very first principal role with ABT, the Don Quixote pas de deux, was also on the Kennedy Center stage. I was just seventeen and it was a very important moment for me.

In 2001, I performed at the Kennedy Center Honors for the first time. A few years later, I was asked to join the Artists Committee for the Honors. To be a part of this committee continues to be a great honor. I feel very much at home on the stage of the Center and it will always hold a special place in my heart.

—Paloma Herrera

PALOMA HERRERA is a Principal Dancer with American Ballet Theatre.

Lebanon's Caracalla Dance Theatre performs Knights of Moon *as part of the Center's 2009 Arabesque: Arts of the Arab World festival.*

modern dance of forms and styles that originated in Africa, as well as the genius of African-American choreographers in preserving, advancing, and extrapolating on those influences. Tracking the African presence in the New World from the earliest days of slavery, the festival placed dance squarely in the stream of African-American creativity that began bubbling in earnest in the 1920s.

"These choreographers have created powerful works that have shattered stereotypes, documented vibrant cultural traditions, and changed the face of dance upon the world stage," Alicia Adams, Kennedy Center Vice President for International Programming and Dance, wrote in the program. "Collectively, their artistry has given birth to an exquisite fusion of ballet, modern dance, jazz, and other distinctive styles of movement and rhythm that both mirror the improvisatory nature of jazz music and also speak to America's spiritual, social, and political soul."

Honoring thirty-two dance leaders past and present, the five-day event hailed Asadata Dafora, Pearl Primus, and Katherine Dunham for their pioneering work in the thirties and forties and their crucial function as role models for and fosterers of coming generations of choreographers and dancers. Those generations were represented in the program: Alvin Ailey and Judith Jamison, Talley Beatty, Arthur Mitchell, and Donald McKayle. The bill also included latter-day avatars Ronald K. Brown, Chuck Davis, Garth Fagan, Rennie Harris, Koffi Koko, Dianne McIntyre, Bebe Miller, Bill T. Jones, Tamango, Jawole Willa Jo Zollar,

The Mark Morris Dance Group performs at the Center in 2009, in Mozart Dances, *as part of the Modern Masters celebration.*

and Paradigm, the age-defying trio of Carmen de Lavallade, Gus Solomons, Jr., and Dudley Williams. Rounding out the festival were performances by regional repertory companies established by African-American women: Dallas Black Dance Theatre, founded by Ann Williams; Dayton Contemporary Dance Company, founded by the late Jeraldyne Blunden; Philadelphia Dance Company (Philadanco), founded by Joan Myers Brown; Denver-based Cleo Parker Robinson Dance, and Lula Washington Dance Theatre of Los Angeles.

While it was not the exclusive focus, dance was a major component of another significant festival on the Center's calendar. The Japan festival delivered a number of important dance performances. Dancer-choreographer Jo Kanamori and company performed the world premiere of *Noism 08: NINA materialize sacrifice*, a special edition of their work, which merges contemporary dance with ballet. Famed *butoh* company Sankai Juku danced *Kinkan Shonen*, the hypnotic piece that made the troupe's reputation in the United States. In a Washington premiere, Akira Kasai performed his solo *Pollen Revolution*.

Dance at the Center has crossed national boundaries, has defied tradition, and has challenged audiences. From ballet to modern, from Europe to Asia, dancers have given American audiences a fascinating view of the depth and breadth of their art form.

Coming of Age

For me the Center represents not only our nation's cultural coming of age, but also my personal coming of age. Having trained and grown up in Washington, I awaited the Center's opening much as I awaited the start of my professional life. During the same week, I participated in the very first Opera House performance—Beatrix Cenci, with Washington Opera—and attended the world premiere of Bernstein's Mass. I knew then that the Center would house countless historic performances, and dreamed of being part of them. My dreams came true for twenty years, and for another twenty I've watched dancers come of age at this place where so much of our art form's history has been made and continues to be made.

—Kevin McKenzie

KEVIN MCKENZIE, Artistic Director of American Ballet Theatre, performed many times at the Center with Joffrey Ballet and with ABT. He closed out his performing career at the Center as a dancer with The Washington Ballet.

Antal Doráti conducts the National Symphony Orchestra. The Hungarian-born composer and conductor was the Orchestra's music director and principal conductor from 1970 to 1977.

III. IN TUNE WITH THE TIMES

The National Symphony Orchestra's (NSO) presence is a given at many state occasions, inaugurations, holiday celebrations, and other events of significance. The Orchestra has always been a fixture at the Kennedy Center, as resident symphony starting in 1971 and since 1986 as part of the Center organization. The 100-member NSO gives some 175 concerts annually, including classical subscription series, pops concerts, and a rigorous educational program. Through the Hechinger Fund, the Orchestra has commissioned more than sixty works representing the diversity of American composition. Long before the Center opened, the Orchestra was developing the hallmarks by which it still is known: familiarity as a hometown pillar, capacity for growth, and dedication to public service.

Hans Kindler founded the Orchestra. The Rotterdam-born cellist made his Washington conducting debut in 1928 at the Library of Congress. Three years later, having recruited sponsors, subscribers, and some seventy-five musicians, he debuted the National Symphony Orchestra at Constitution Hall. Guest performers included Vladimir Horowitz, Josef Hofmann, Walter Gieseking, Arthur Rubinstein, Rudolf Serkin, and Kirsten Flagstad. Igor Stravinsky conducted the NSO, as did Georges Enesco and Bruno Walter. In 1935, Kindler and colleagues began giving free summer concerts at the Watergate (not the building complex but a riverside spot downstream from where the Center now stands). The Orchestra played aboard a barge while listeners sat on the curved bank of steps beside Memorial Bridge or bobbed on the Potomac in canoes (as seen in the Cary Grant/Sophia Loren movie *Houseboat*). These shows prefigured the Mall concerts that have made millions of television viewers fans of the National Symphony Orchestra.

In 1949, principal cellist and assistant conductor Howard Mitchell succeeded Kindler. During more than twenty years leading the Orchestra, Mitchell tirelessly promoted classical music and, by association, the NSO. He started Young Peoples' Concerts to instill in youthful listeners a love for classical music. Among the world-famous guest conductors at regular performances were Sir Thomas Beecham, Leopold Stokowski, and Pierre Monteux. Soloists making American debuts with the NSO under Mitchell included pianists Philippe Entremont and Vladimir Ashkenazy and, in 1956, cellist Mstislav Rostropovich. In 1959, Mitchell took the Orchestra on its first international tour: sixty-eight concerts in nineteen countries in Latin America and South America. In 1967, he led the group's first European tour. One proud hometown highlight between foreign tours was the Orchestra's appearance at President Kennedy's inauguration.

A splendid musician's-eye view of the Concert Hall shows its orchestra, parterre. and tier seats illuminated by crystal chandeliers, a gift from Norway.

Antal Doráti became music director in 1970. Four decades of conducting had left him nothing if not bold. Touring the unfinished Kennedy Center with Roger Stevens, Doráti insisted that the NSO be the Center's resident orchestra.

The season that it opened the Concert Hall, the NSO also welcomed guest soloist Ruggiero Ricci and guest conductor Leopold Stokowski, and in between, on cello, Mstislav Rostropovich. Soon after, Rostropovich gave a Concert Hall recital with his wife, soprano Galina Vishnevskaya.

Doráti and the NSO presented many works and gave numerous Washington premieres, including Burton's "Fanfare," La Montaine's "Wilderness Journal," Penderecki's "Dies Irae," and Kodály's "Old Hungarian Soldiers' Tunes." Doráti's enthusiasm for American composers led to world-premiere performances of Schuman's "The Young Dead Soldiers," "Casey at the Bat," and his Symphony No. 10, "American Muse." The NSO also debuted Miklós Rózsa's "Tripartita," Gunther Schuller's "Concerto for Orchestra," and Ulysses Kay's "Western Paradise."

In an autobiography written after he left Washington, Doráti summed up his feelings for the Center: "It is not only the face but also the spirit of Washington that the Kennedy Center has changed. It represents the greatest success of its kind I have ever encountered. From the day of its opening, it has upgraded the cultural appetite and taste of the city, given it a focus, and, so to speak, a 'digestive tract.' It is well on the way to increasing its influence, and because of its existence one can now seriously consider Washington as, in the very near future, a potential national and even international center of culture."

The 1970s were a financially challenging time for arts organizations and orchestras. Tour funding was scarce. Once the Center opened, it hosted most of the Orchestra's appearances through early 1976. Doráti's strenuous efforts to improve the Orchestra and its repertoire while heightening public awareness of the NSO poised the Orchestra for its next phase, which would bring more attention in the decade to come than anyone could have predicted.

Slava to the Podium

In 1975, Antal Doráti was seven years into a planned ten-year stay with the NSO. He also was at loggerheads with the Orchestra's board. That March, Mstislav Rostropovich, by now a towering figure on the music scene who had left Russia rather than tolerate continued abuse for his efforts on behalf of human rights, made an electrifying appearance with the NSO as guest conductor. Talks ensued, and within weeks the Orchestra named the cellist as its music director. His arrival in 1977 changed the trajectory of Rostropovich's career and the Orchestra's. He led the NSO until 1996.

Slava ("Glory" in Russian), as everyone close to Rostropovich knew him, reveled in his work and in his life. *Time* magazine put him on its cover. Audiences greeted him with standing ovations and cheers. Willing to barter his cachet as probably the world's best and most famous cellist, he drew guest conductors to the NSO podium in exchange for agreeing to play in their halls, with their orchestras. Even critics who disdained his technique noted that

Rostropovich's idiosyncratic élan could lead to golden moments. "You must play for the love of music," Slava said. "Perfect technique is not as important as making music from the heart."

Slava's worldwide fame attached itself to the Orchestra. The Orchestra rose to the challenge, stepping to a new level. Rostropovich brought in guest conductors Leonard Bernstein, Seiji Ozawa, Erich Leinsdorf, Claudio Abbado, Lorin Maazel, Zubin Mehta, and Leonard Slatkin. His choices of music ranged from American music (not only popular works but many that had been all but forgotten), to material resonantly Russian: Tchaikovsky, Prokofiev, Shostakovich, to name a few.

In 1979, the Orchestra revived its tradition of free holiday concerts, staging them not at the Watergate Steps but on the west lawn of the Capitol. These events on Memorial Day, the Fourth of July, and Labor Day, drew huge crowds, and PBS carried them live on television. They have become a much-beloved tradition, not only for Washingtonians and the thousands of other concertgoers who pack the lawns, but for viewers and listeners around the country and the world.

Bringing It All Back Home—A New Decade

Under Mstislav Rostropovich the Orchestra continued to gain fans and to advance its reputation. The Orchestra celebrated its fiftieth anniversary in 1980 with a gala concert featuring Rostropovich and Vishnevskaya, along with Isaac Stern, Leonard Bernstein,

Two of the NSO's former music directors, Mstislav Rostropovich (left), and Leonard Slatkin (right), enjoy a warm moment together in front of the camera.

and Jean-Pierre Rampal. That season was heavy on birthday concerts. One featured Stern as a soloist to celebrate his sixtieth birthday, in the company of Rostropovich, Eugene Ormandy, Zubin Mehta, Julius Rudel, and Leonard Slatkin. A month later came Aaron Copland's eightieth. The birthday boy, Bernstein, and Rostropovich each conducted in a concert taped for broadcast as the first program of the PBS series *Kennedy Center Tonight!*

Besides investing the Orchestra with an international glamour, Rostropovich remade its sound. "He turned the orchestra into his own enormous instrument . . . its basic sound changed noticeably," Ted Libbey wrote in *The National Symphony Orchestra.*

During the 1970s, the cost of running a symphony orchestra had ballooned. The Orchestra pressed on, touring nationally and internationally. But by the mid-1980s, the NSO, never overendowed, ran into money trouble. At the same time, costs were preventing

Slava delights the audience as he conducts the NSO during a performance at the Center.

President George H.W. Bush and Mrs. Bush greet Slava on a 1988 visit to the White House as National Symphony Orchestra members look on.

other orchestras from touring. In 1986, talks rooted in mutual need led to the Orchestra affiliating with the Center, a relationship rich with mutual benefits.

Orchestral Maneuvers— The Baton Passes to Slatkin

The Orchestra began its innovative American Residency program in 1992. The Residency program has taken the Orchestra to more than twenty states. A mix of exchanges, training, and commissions, each residency focuses on a state's musical influences while sharing all elements of classical symphonic music. In a residency, the entire Orchestra, small ensembles of members, and individual musicians bring their skills to American places that never or rarely have seen or heard a live performance of classical music. Residencies make available rich and varied schedules of performances. Thanks to generous support, principally from the Center and the U.S. Department of Education, revenues from these events go to local arts organizations. Residency presentations have drawn attendance of nearly four hundred thousand.

In 1993, to celebrate the anniversary of Tchaikovsky's death, Rostropovich and the NSO performed in Moscow's Red Square—the first orchestra to do so.

In 1994, Rostropovich stepped down as music director, accepting the position of Lifetime Conductor Laureate. He made good on that title, returning occasionally to take the podium.

Los Angeles–born Leonard Slatkin became music director in 1996. While Slava left big shoes to fill, Slatkin boasted an impressive résumé in his own right: artistic director and conductor for the New York Youth Symphony, music advisor for the New Orleans Symphony, and music director for the St. Louis Symphony Orchestra. Besides bringing more American material to the Orchestra's repertoire, he also steered the NSO through the gutting and refurbishment of the Concert Hall. At the 1997 rededication, Slatkin led the Orchestra in performing his own composition, *Housewarming*, before a capacity audience that included President Bill Clinton and Mrs. Clinton. Slatkin also took the Orchestra on reputation-enhancing tours of Europe.

Slava and the NSO perform for an audience of approximately 10,000 in Moscow's Red Square during their 1993 concert on the anniversary of the Russian composer Tchaikovsky's death. This performance, the NSO's second with Slava in Russia, was the first orchestral concert in Red Square and was "an emotionally charged event."

Enter Eschenbach

As the twenty-first century began, the National Symphony Orchestra continued to explore new territory. Leonard Slatkin, credited with reenergizing the NSO since his arrival as music director designate in 1994, commissioned scores of new works by American composers that helped the Orchestra gain a reputation for taking chances. During 2000–2008, the Orchestra operated the National Conducting Institute, which Slatkin founded, to nurture young conductors, including John Clanton and Mark Mandarano. In 2004, the Center announced that Slatkin would step down at the end of the 2007–2008 season.

After Slatkin's departure, Iván Fischer, as principal conductor, guided the Orchestra through an interim preceding Christoph Eschenbach's arrival as music director in 2010. Eschenbach, a noted conductor and pianist, previously led the Houston Symphony Orchestra, the Philadelphia Orchestra, the NDR Symphony Orchestra in Hamburg, Germany, the Tonhalle Orchestra Zurich, and L'Orchestre de Paris. He was known for his dedication to the musicians he led and his attention to musical detail. In addition to being music director of the National Symphony Orchestra, he was also named music director of the John F. Kennedy Center for the Performing Arts, signaling an expectation to integrate the NSO even more thoroughly into the larger Center calendar. For example, the Maximum India Festival featured three NSO programs that reflected and enhanced themes of the festival, including an NSO-commissioned world premiere from *tabla* player-composer Zakir Hussain.

Founded in times of duress, the NSO has matured into a strong and energetic musical organization whose deep roots in Washington have helped it to become a national and international presence. As the record of the last forty years shows, the Center has been a huge part of that maturation, and the Orchestra has conferred on the Center a lasting reputation as the home of a great symphony orchestra.

Never Just Another Night

Playing music for events at the Kennedy Center for twenty-five years, from solo piano to leading a full band, I've never had just another night at work. The audience is excited to be there. The acoustics are glorious. The Center provides superb instruments. The people you work with are wonderful. It's always a thrill and an honor, whether onstage accompanying a star or providing background music in some intimate space.

—Glenn Pearson

GLENN PEARSON, a Washington, D.C., pianist, leads the dance band Floating Opera, performs solo and in small ensembles, and appears with Rock & Soul Revue WMD.

Music in the Upper Room—Chamber Music

The Orchestra wasn't the only source of classical music at the Center. Chamber music has always been an important part of the musical offerings. The 1971 season featured a well-received chamber music performance in the Concert Hall by the Istomin-Stern-Rose Trio. The next season brought such luminaries as the New York String Orchestra, the Guarneri Quartet with Rudolf Serkin, and the Chamber Music Society of Lincoln Center. In subsequent years, festivals honoring Mozart, Haydn, and Handel included much chamber music.

In 1979, a three million dollar gift from Japan transformed a storage space above the Eisenhower Theater into the Terrace Theater, designed by Philip Johnson and John Burgee Architects. The room became the home at the Center of chamber music, which was featured in the inaugural Terrace Theater performance by the Tokyo String Quartet. The genre retains pride of place there, while additional presentations are always possible at Millennium Stage and elsewhere in the building. Besides its role in presenting chamber music, the Terrace Theater is the Center's Off-Broadway, serving multiple forms and missions, such as jazz performances, small ensembles, and plays needing a more intimate, nurturing setting.

Honoring Abe Fortas

Chamber music's presence at the Center deepened in 1983 when, to honor the late Abe Fortas, former Supreme Court Justice and amateur musician, his friends Isaac Stern and Eugene Istomin gave a concert. The proceeds endowed a fund supporting the genre at the Center. As it has grown, the Fortas fund has allowed programmers to present world-class chamber music, including frequent appearances by the Kalichstein-Laredo-Robinson Trio. Made up of pianist Joseph Kalichstein, violinist Jaime Laredo, and cellist Sharon Robinson, the trio, which debuted at the White House during President Carter's inaugural festivities, is legendary for its intensity and lyricism. Its appearances—such as a three-concert Brahms Festival have entered the Center's performance lore.

Beloved both by Center audiences and music aficionados the world over, Sharon Robinson (left), Jaime Laredo (center), and Joseph Kalichstein (right) have played together since 1977, frequently appearing at the Center.

CHRISTOPH ESCHENBACH

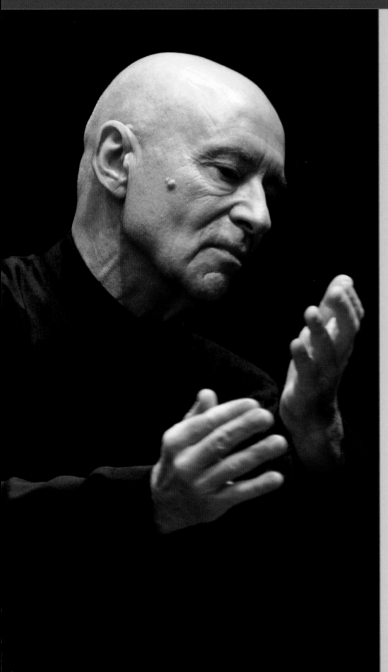

By the time Christoph Eschenbach was announced as Music Director Designate beginning in the 2010–11 season, he was already renowned worldwide as a pianist and conductor. A native of Breslau, Germany, he won several piano competitions in his early years. He was signed by a major classical music label in 1964 and began the first of dozens of recordings in his five-decade long career.

Mentored by conducting legends George Szell and Herbert von Karajan, Eschenbach was named Chief Conductor of Zurich's Tonhalle Orchestra in 1982 where he later served as artistic director. Houston Symphony welcomed him to his first American post in 1988, a wonderful relationship that lasted for nearly a dozen years. He also served as music director of the Ravinia festival in Chicago and artistic director of the prestigious Schleswig-Holstein Music Festival in northern Germany. Eschenbach was appointed music director of the Philadelphia Orchestra—one of the "big-five" orchestras in the United States—in 2004.

Eschenbach takes great pleasure in discovering and mentoring young artists, many of whom have gained international prominence. At the opening of his first season as music director at the National Symphony Orchestra Ball, longtime protégées and collaborators Renée Fleming and Lang Lang were there to perform and celebrate the occasion.

Eschenbach is renowned for his generous mentoring and commitment to the development of young musicians.

Eschenbach has a strong commitment not only to the orchestras he leads, but to the individual musicians. At the Kennedy Center, he has performed free concerts on the Millennium Stage that highlighted the talents of several orchestra members.

Eschenbach himself has said, "The joy of the interactions among the various art forms makes the Kennedy Center a unique and special place, and the collaborative nature of the relationships is particularly pleasing. We work together."

Christoph Eschenbach, the Center's and NSO's music director, conducts the National Symphony Orchestra at an August 2009 rehearsal.

Yo-Yo Ma has a long history of performance at the Center—he played there as a teen and has appeared there often during his celebrated career—and in 2011 he was named a Kennedy Center Honoree.

Funding for the Fortas Chamber Music Concert Series was augmented in 1996 by a generous bequest from the Justice's widow, Carolyn Agger. Enhanced by the Fortas endowment and amplified by Agger's generosity, the Center's commitment to chamber music has encouraged repertoires and artists less focused on the bottom line than on the best music possible. In 1997, Joseph Kalichstein was named Artistic Advisor on Chamber Music and Artistic Director of the Fortas Chamber Music Concerts, a position he still holds in addition to his work as a principal in the Center's Kalichstein-Laredo-Robinson Trio.

Advancing Chamber Music

In 2007–08, financial assistance from Agger funding enabled the Center to present the Alban Berg Quartet on that group's final tour of the United States, a coup of the sort usually out of the reach of a hall as intimate as the 513-seat Terrace Theater. "This endowment gave us a tremendous floor," Kalichstein said. "It provides a lot of artistic freedom.

We are very lucky to have it. The music and the series existed before the gift and would have continued, but the Agger gift does give us lots of breathing room."

In January 2011, as part of the Center series The Presidency of John F. Kennedy: A 50th Anniversary Celebration the Kalichstein-Laredo-Robinson Trio participated in a commemoration of Pablo Casals's legendary East Room concert. Joining the chamber music trio were pianist Emanuel Ax and cellist Yo-Yo Ma. The event had musical and historical resonances, since Ma had performed as a seven-year-old as part of a fund-raiser during the Center's beginning. The 2011 program reprised the one Casals chose in 1961 for President and Mrs. Kennedy and their guests. The latter-day ensemble performed works by Couperin, Schumann, and Mendelssohn, adding a piece by Beethoven. And, invoking Casals's impromptu encore fifty years before, the evening closed with his beloved hymn to freedom, "Song of the Birds."

The Rise of Jazz

Music is more than the classical canon. Music changes, adapts, evolves. The development of a culture's music can provide fascinating insights into the culture itself. One of the more interesting musical journeys is that of jazz, a quintessentially American musical art form. While grand symphonies might have been composed for royalty, jazz was composed by and for the common man. Precision is a point of pride among classical virtuosos, while jazz musicians prize their ability to improvise. Innovation, improvisation, creativity, passion: Jazz provides a fascinating glimpse at American culture and American identity.

Jazz has always played the Kennedy Center. The original Jazz Advisory Panel included David Baker, Julian "Cannonball" Adderley, John Lewis, Dizzy Gillespie, and Clark Terry. Some of those aces appeared in the 1971–72 Founding Artists Series, as did Count Basie, Duke Ellington, Bill Evans, Gil Evans, Earl Hines, Tony Bennett, and others.

For years, the Center itself programmed jazz intermittently, in addition to shows presented by others. Later major jazz festivals filled the building with performers and crowds.

Taylor to the Fore

In 1994, the Center named Dr. Billy Taylor artistic adviser (and later artistic director) for jazz, an appointment that lent programming more structure and energy. A pianist, composer, educator, and radio host, Dr. Taylor had been doing a New York-based series combining interviews with and performances by jazz notables. He moved this venture south, where it became *NPR's Billy Taylor's Jazz at the Kennedy Center*. Featuring the Billy Taylor Trio and guests, the show aired from 1994 to 2001, and led to more musical collaboration between the Center and the network. NPR's annual New Year's Eve broadcast of live performances from around the country often included shows at the Center. WBGO-FM of Newark, New Jersey, produced NPR's *Jazz Set with Dee Dee Bridgewater*, a performance series carried monthly by many stations.

In 1996, Dr. Taylor established the Kennedy Center Mary Lou Williams Women in Jazz Festival to showcase the contributions of female instrumentalists and to present a lifetime achievement award named for the late pianist, composer, and arranger. The Center has emerged as the premier presenter of women's jazz festivals, increasing exposure for new and established artists.

A year later, the Center and the U.S. Information Agency (and its successor, the U.S. Department of State's Bureau of Educational and Cultural Affairs) began collaborating on the Jazz Ambassadors program, which annually sent jazz groups to represent American music overseas through 2005. Participating performers came from all over the country and were chosen by competitive audition. Groups toured for four to six

Jazz artist Dee Dee Bridgewater belts out a tune in a 2007 performance with the Terence Blanchard Quintet. Bridgewater is closely associated with the Center; her monthly Jazz Set NPR series from the Center is widely heard.

weeks at a time, appearing in scores of countries not often visited by American musicians. In addition to their performances, Jazz Ambassadors conducted master classes and gave lecture-recitals for local musicians. Sadly, Dr. Taylor died on December 28, 2010.

Jazz in a New Century

Over the decades, jazz bookings at the Center have multiplied dramatically. They now number about sixty per year, not counting jazz acts appearing on the Millennium Stage. Since 2002, the Kennedy Center Jazz Club has been the setting for more than a dozen acts a year.

One epic jazz event at the Center was 2007's Jazz in Our Time, a seven-day celebration ranging the length and breadth of the form and echoing Art Kane's legendary 1958 photograph, made in Harlem, of an earlier era's leading jazz icons.

Benny Golson (saxophone) and John Clayton (bass) perform at the 2007 Jazz in Our Time gala.

Dr. Bill Taylor was a jazz legend. A brilliant pianist, composer, and educator, Taylor's musical career spanned six decades. During that time, he worked with some of the true legends of American jazz, including Charlie Parker, Dizzy Gillespie, Miles Davis, and Art Tatum. In addition to being a fantastic musician, he also composed 350 songs.

But Taylor was not content with simply playing music, or creating new music. He was also an influential educator, bringing jazz to a wider audience. Early in his career, Taylor became the Musical Director for NBC's *The Subject Is Jazz*, the first ever television series to focus entirely on jazz. A believer in the importance of education, Taylor received his Masters and Doctorate in Music Education from the University of Massachusetts at Amherst and served as the Duke Ellington Fellow at Yale University.

For his musical accomplishments, Taylor was showered with awards, including two Peabody Awards, an Emmy, and a Grammy. He was also the recipient of the National Medal of Arts, and was elected to the Hall of Fame for the International Association for Jazz Education. Taylor passed away in December 2010, at the age of 89.

Above: Dr. Bill Taylor's eloquent voice educated millions of listeners about jazz. His long radio and television career was capped with the performance and interview series Billy Taylor's Jazz at the Kennedy Center, which debuted on NPR in 1994 and ran until 2002. Right: Taylor shares an onstage laugh with fellow jazz musician, Jon Faddis, a world-renowned trumpet player.

Taylor, on the piano, leads the Morgan State University Choir at the 2007 Jazz in Our Time festival.

From left to right: Frank Wess, Phil Woods, James Moody, and Jimmy Heath lend their saxophones to the CHJO in the Jazz in Our Time festival.

In addition to a Family Theater show in honor of Marian McPartland's birthday, Jazz in Our Time included Millennium Stage performances by artists representing the many stylistic mansions of jazz, from ragtime to fusion to hip-hop crossover.

The week's keystone, a Concert Hall performance hosted by James Earl Jones, featured vocalist Nancy Wilson, violinist Regina Carter, drummer T. S. Monk, pianists Dave Brubeck, Cyrus Chestnut, and Michel Legrand, trumpeter Jon Faddis, and saxophonists James Moody, Phil Woods, and Frank Wess, with the Morgan State University Choir. The Clayton Brothers Quintet, the Billy Taylor Trio, the Wynton Marsalis Quintet, and the Clayton-Hamilton Jazz Orchestra also appeared. Many of these performers received Living Legend Jazz Awards, also conferred on Abbey Lincoln, Louis Bellson, Ornette Coleman, Billy Taylor, Buddy DeFranco, Paquito D'Rivera, Sir John Dankworth, Dame Cleo Laine, Dave Brubeck and others—a total of thirty-three immortals honored in their time rather than after their passing. The proceeds

Making an Impact

It's been amazing working with the Kennedy Center because of their commitment to the arts. Their work runs the gamut in the art world. It's not one particular thing. Classical music. Art. Jazz. Dance. Visual arts. It's remarkable all the things they've done. Their record for success has been unmatched in the world of art.

And it's not just about the performances. It's also what they do with the community. Arts can have a big effect on people. I was doing some teaching gigs, and the teachers told us about what happened when we were teaching a master class. One of the kids there was a bit of a problem kid, but after the class, our drummer gave him his sticks, and his teacher said that since then, he hasn't given them any trouble at all.

One of the reasons the arts is so important is because art makes us delve into our psyche, delve into our own insecurities and our own foibles. In that abstract world, there is universal communication that goes beyond language. When we react to those things, we see how we are all connected. In that moment, that's where the arts can bring down barriers.

—Terence Blanchard

TERENCE BLANCHARD is a four-time Grammy-winning trumpeter, bandleader, composer, arranger, and film score composer. Since 2000, he served as the Artistic Director of the Thelonious Monk Institute of Jazz.

closed with a screening of *A Great Day in Harlem*, Jean Bach's acclaimed documentary about the making of Kane's famous photo.

Jazz programming coups have included salutes to Ella Fitzgerald and Lionel Hampton, a rare reunion of all the members of the musical Marsalis family, shows celebrating Dr. Taylor's eightieth birthday and the jazz heritage of Washington, D.C., performances by Benny Golson and Shirley Horn, and a Terrace Theater appearance by Harry Connick, Jr. and Branford Marsalis.

An Education in Jazz

Education is a key part of jazz at the Center. Its centerpiece is Betty Carter's Jazz Ahead program, which grew out of the late singer's interest in developing new generations of musicians by staffing her bands with younger players so they could absorb the traditions she knew and improve their skills in a real-world setting.

First formalized at the Brooklyn Academy of Music, Jazz Ahead moved to the Center in 1997 at Dr. Taylor's invitation. The rigorous workshops, open each spring to young musicians from around the United States, charge no tuition. Besides having instrumental or vocal chops, workshop enrollees must be composers, too. With jazz professionals guiding them, each workshop's twenty participants perform and critique one another's charts as well as play on the Millennium Stage. Some shows are aired by NPR's *Jazzset*. Jazz Ahead alumni include pianist and MacArthur Grant recipient Jason Moran, and the Jazz Club's Discovery Series often features Jazz Ahead alumni.

Center efforts in jazz education also include distance learning and performing arts programs at George Washington University and at Hylton High School in Prince William County, Virginia. The Education Department continually adds jazz master classes, courses, and lectures, and community partnerships so schools can have more jazz content.

Dee Dee Bridgewater hosted the 13th annual Mary Lou Williams Women in Jazz Festival in 2009.

Photographer John Abbott references Art Kane's famous 1958 photo "A Great Day in Harlem" with "A Great Day in Washington,"
a group portrait of jazz legends at the Center's 2007 Jazz in Our Time celebration,
Left to right, 1st Row: Clark Terry, Frank Foster, Curtis Fuller, Bill Taylor, Jimmy Scott, Louie Bellson, Marian McPartland, Donald Byrd;
2nd: James Moody, Jimmy Heath, Barry Harris, Nancy Wilson, Benny Golson, Ornette Coleman, Toshiko Akiyoshi, Chick Corea;
3rd: Phil Woods, Chico Hamilton, Buddy DeFranco, George Russel, Freddie Hubbard, Gerald Wilson, Frank Wess, Cleo Laine;
4th: Al Jerreau, Jon Jendricks, Ahmad Jamal, Dave Brubeck, Wynton Marsalis, David Baker, Paquito D'Rivera, John Dankworth, Michael Legrand

MARTA ISTOMIN

Noted arts administrator and fundraiser Marta Istomin spent a decade as Artistic Director at the Center.

Marta Istomin's training for her work as the Center's Artistic Director from 1980 until 1990 was her life.

Marta Montañez Martínez left her native Puerto Rico to attend music school in New York City, a path that led her to meet, study with, and marry legendary musician Pablo Casals. Helping the cellist with his festivals in Prades, France, and then with his work founding the Casals Festival, the Symphony Orchestra of Puerto Rico, and the Conservatory of Music in San Juan, Puerto Rico, she learned the intricacies of arts management. Washington lawyer and amateur violinist Abe Fortas, who served on the Casals Festival Board, became a close friend of the couple. After Casals's death in 1973, his widow ran the arts organization named for him. A string instruction program for youngsters that she established has produced most of the Puerto Rico Symphony's string players. She also taught cello as a visiting professor at Curtis Institute of Music in Philadelphia, Pennsylvania.

In 1975, Mrs. Casals married pianist Eugene Istomin, who often performed at the Center with the National Symphony Orchestra and the Washington Performing Arts Society. The Istomins' circle included Fortas, who served on the U.S. Supreme Court from 1965 to 1969, and other capital figures such as Roger Stevens.

After Mrs. Istomin resigned from the Casals Festival Organization, Fortas encouraged her to keep using her skills. In 1979, when Martin Feinstein left the Center, Fortas encouraged Istomin to consider replacing him. Eventually he brought Roger Stevens to make an offer. Enticed by the prospect of developing programs reflecting the best music nationally and internationally, Istomin agreed to become artistic director.

At the Center, Istomin oversaw all non-theatrical presentations. "Roger Stevens was passionate about the theater programs, and for the most part, he left the rest to me—music, dance, festivals," she said. "Roger was tough but fair. If he believed in you and you believed in what you wanted to do, he would back you. He would take chances. He approved my budgets, and his only questions were, 'Is it important that we do this, and is it high quality?' I didn't feel that we always had to have big names, but that we did have to present quality."

Under Istomin, the Terrace Theater presented a range of performers, including multiple series devoted to piano, string quartets, American composers, violin and cello sonatas, art songs, and chamber orchestra, along with a Musicians from Marlboro series and a jazz series. Each mounted at least five concerts per season. One series begun during that era continues. To honor Abe Fortas, who died in 1983, his friends Eugene Istomin and Isaac Stern gave a concert. The proceeds established the Fortas Chamber Music Series. The same year, to mark the twentieth anniversary of John F. Kennedy's death, the Center organized concerts celebrating his life.

Mrs. Istomin's work at the Center renewed a long-standing friendship with Mstislav Rostropovich. Supplementing the Orchestra's presence, she scheduled major orchestras from around the world, such as the Amsterdam Concertgebouw. In the late 1980s, she arranged for the Deutsche Oper Berlin, bringing a full production and roster of soloists, chorus, and orchestra, presented two complete cycles of Wagner's *Ring of the Nibelung*.

Istomin arranged partnerships with such entities as the Theater Chamber Players, Young Concert Artists, and visiting Latin American groups. Her interests also included dance and theater. Complementing the performances, educational and outreach programs deepened and intensified in all disciplines.

Istomin was integral to early efforts to benefit the Opera House renovation. One concert, a black-tie event in 1983, featured Plácido Domingo with Julius Rudel conducting the NSO, and set the standard for fund-raisers at the Center. She also lent her energies to luncheons where she advocated eloquently for the performing arts—and for the Center as a beneficiary of guests' generosity.

As an antidote to the capital's snooze-inducing summer, Istomin began to schedule vigorously during that season. Summers now included chamber orchestra presentations such as Mostly Mozart, the St. Paul Chamber Orchestra, and other ensembles from around the U.S. International companies such as Japan's Grand Kabuki appeared, as did the Peking Opera.

Istomin tried to be present at performances by artists she brought to the Center's stages, an effort she saw as managerial due diligence. "It was never an imposition," she said. "I was always supported by a dedicated group of people who felt as I did—that artists deserve to have the best conditions possible for their performances and that they value your effort and commitment to them. And this usually results in the best possible performance for the public."

Late in 1990 Istomin decided to leave the Center. This desolated Slava Rostropovich, but soon he was asking for her help with a festival he had begun in Evian, France. "'France?' I said. 'Slava, how am I going to do that?'" she said. "He said,

The Kennedy Center Opera House's chandelier was a gift from Austria.

`You will do fine.' I agreed to help for one year." She served as General Director of the Evian Festival for eight years, and then again called it a day.

She thought.

Earlier, the Manhattan School of Music had offered Istomin its presidency, an overture the school then repeated. This time she accepted, signing a three-year contract. She stayed thirteen years. Eugene Istomin died in 2003. Not long after, Marta Istomin moved back to Washington. From her living room, she can see the Center, on which she has emphatic views.

"The Kennedy Center serves the nation's capital, the country, and the world. Washington's global significance enhances the awareness of performances of great quality at the Center," Istomin said. "The Center was built because we Americans believe in the arts and we believe that culture is very important for the quality of life. I found as Artistic Director that the Center was very important to artists and to smaller companies of quality, like the Houston Ballet, Ballet West, Hubbard Street Dance, and others. To perform at the Center meant great prestige, a 'seal of approval,' as it were. The Kennedy Center was meant to be an artistic home for all top quality performers, whether famous or not."

The world-famous Peking Opera made its U.S. debut under Istomin's tenure, in the 1985-86 season.

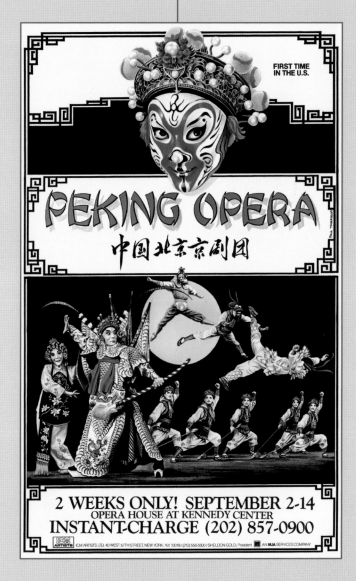

115

IV. OPERA IN ACTION

The Washington National Opera (WNO) has a long history at the Center and in the capital. A premiere 1971 performance at the Opera House of Alberto Ginastera's *Beatrix Cenci* as well as Beverly Sills's appearance that same year as Gineura in Handel's *Ariodante* led to a four-decade residency and to formal affiliation in July 2011.

Founded in 1956 as the Opera Society of Washington, the Washington National Opera has showcased the works of the field's most popular and creative minds, including Ginastera, Frederick Delius, Gian Carlo Menotti, Igor Stravinsky, Paul Hindemith, Samuel Barber, Lee Hoiby, and a host of other modern composers.

The opening of the Center provided the Opera with a fine new setting. The deep Opera House stage made possible extensive productions. The company quickly took to the new space. So did D.C. opera fans.

Some of the more noted Opera productions at the Center included Menotti's *Goya* and Dominick Argento's *The Dream of Valentino*, as well as *Carmen* with famed mezzo-soprano Denyce Graves. The company presented *Turandot* with Eva Marton, the great bass-baritone Samuel Ramey in *Mefistofele*, *Salome* with Maria Ewing, and Barber's *Vanessa*. Other coups were productions of Eugen d'Albert's rarely performed *Tiefland*, the East Coast

Beverly Sills made the first of many Center appearances in 1971, in Handel's rarely staged Ariodante, *one of the three productions that opened the Center. (The other two were Bernstein's* Mass *and Ginastera's* Beatrix Cenci.*)*

Mezzo-soprano Denyce Graves and tenor José Cura appear in a scene from the Washington National Opera 1998 production of Samson et Dalila.

premiere of Argento's *The Aspern Papers*, Leoš Janáček's *The Cunning Little Vixen*, *La Bohème* directed by Menotti, and the American premiere of the Chinese work *Savage Land*. With L'Orchestre de Paris, the company coproduced the Mozart/da Ponte operas, conducted by Daniel Barenboim and staged by Jean-Pierre Ponnelle. With L'Opéra de Monte Carlo, the company produced the Rimsky-Korsakov gem *The Tsar's Bride*, beginning a Russian cycle including *Eugene Onegin* and *Pique Dame*.

A Legend Takes the Helm

Plácido Domingo's long association with the Center stretches back to its very beginnings. He was a founding artist and sang with Martina Arroyo in one of the opening concerts in 1972. Almost twenty-five years later, in 1996, he became General Director of the Washington Opera, with plans to expand the company's activities and enlarge its international presence. Domingo's more colorful accomplishments and productions included José Carreras in Wolf-Ferrari's *Sly*, Mirella Freni in *Fedora* (with Domingo), and Renée Fleming in *Lucrezia Borgia*. Other important performances included José Cura and Denyce Graves in *Samson et Dalila*; Samuel Ramey in *Boris Godunov*; Eva Marton in *Elektra*; Ainhoa Arteta in Puccini's *La Rondine*; Ruggero Raimondi in Piero Faggioni's production of *Don Quichotte*; and *Parsifal* conducted by Heinz Fricke and starring Domingo and an international cast of Wagnerians. In 2010, Domingo announced that he would not be renewing his contract, which expired in 2011.

Affiliation with the Opera

In July 2011, the Center and the Washington National Opera agreed to affiliate, a move offering the Opera more opportunities to stage productions throughout the Center and allowing the Center to count on Opera resources and programming for festivals. The Opera also gained economies of scale, financial security, and participation in the Center's educational program.

"Affiliation will ensure that the Washington area will forever have a strong, vibrant, and world-class opera, and that is a plus for the Kennedy Center, WNO, and lovers of opera everywhere," Center Chairman David M. Rubenstein said. "WNO and the Kennedy Center have always shared a commitment to presenting great opera," Opera President Kenneth Feinberg said. "By formally affiliating, we and our audiences will reap the benefits."

Samuel Ramey, one of the world's foremost bass and bass-baritones, appeared in one of his signature roles as title character in Boito's Mefistofele *at the Center in 1995.*

GEORGES BIZET

Carmen

Nov 8, 10, 12, 14, 16m, 18, 19, 2008

In French with English supertitles

WASHINGTON
NATIONAL
OPERA

Plácido Domingo
General Director

202.295.2400 • 800.US.OPERA
www.dc-opera.org
Kennedy Center Opera House

Left: *José Carreras stars in the title role in the WNO 1999 production of Sly.*

Above: *2008 poster for* Carmen *featuring Denyce Graves.*

Opera at the Kennedy Center

Throughout its forty-year history, the Center has hosted not only Washington National Opera productions but also numerous highly acclaimed opera companies from around the United States and the world. The Center has brought outstanding, unusual productions to the nation's stage, providing opera-hungry audiences with the chance to see historic revivals and debuts as well as premieres and beloved repertory favorites.

In the first decade the Center hosted the first American visits of a number of acclaimed European companies: the Bolshoi Opera, the Berlin Opera, Teatro alla Scala, and the Vienna State Opera, as well as productions by the Berlin Opera, the Paris Opera, and the Rome Piccolo Opera. Distinguished American performances included Houston Grand Opera's 1975 production of American composer Scott Joplin's *Treemonisha*.

The Bolshoi deserves special mention. During the Cold War era of the 1970s, appearances by Soviet artists in the West were rare and difficult to book, and Western audiences eagerly anticipated the Bolshoi's international tours. In 1976, the Bolshoi Opera made its U.S. premiere with *Boris Godunov* in a two-week engagement that also included performances of *Eugene Onegin*, *The Queen of Spades*, *War and Peace*, and *The Gambler* as part of the Center's celebration of the nation's bicentennial. Often, the Bolshoi's appearances at the Center—and sometimes the existence of the tours themselves—were due to the expertise and connections of the Center's executive director Martin Feinstein, who had worked with Sol Hurok, one of theater's great impresarios, in New York. Hurok's organization produced or co-produced the tours, and with Feinstein at the Center, the Center and the Bolshoi Opera and Ballet enjoyed a connection that has continued to benefit the company and American audiences for decades.

In the Center's earliest years, New York City Opera had a close association. From the Center's very first season in 1972, through 1979, the New York City Opera mounted annual productions there. Julius Rudel was named the Center's first music director and conducted many performances, including *Ariodante* in the Center's first week—the first time that work had been staged in America. He later went on to become general director of the New York City Opera. Beverly Sills, who starred in those early *Ariodante* performances, made her final appearance onstage at the Center in Rossini's *The Turk in Italy* in 1979.

New Yorkers were never absent from the stage for long. In 1980, the Metropolitan Opera of New York staged its first work at the Center, Donizetti's *L'Elisir d'Amore*, directed by James Levine and starring Luciano Pavarotti. The Met returned several times in the 1980s, with notable productions including Zandonai's *Francesca da Rimini* and Puccini's *Tosca*, both featuring Plácido Domingo, in 1984.

The opera program continued strongly throughout the 1980s. Prominent pieces at the Center that decade include the spectacular Peking Opera's *Monkey King Fights 18 Lo Hans*, the Opera Orchestra of New York's performance of *Rienzi*, and productions by La Gran Scena Opera.

Later that decade, together with

Eva Marton appears as Princess Turandot in WNO's production of Puccini's opera of the same name in 1992. Marton is a renowned interpreter of the role.

"A HEROIC OPERA FOR AN UNHEROIC AGE..."
—*Time*

The John F. Kennedy Center for the Performing Arts,
Brooklyn Academy of Music,
Houston Grand Opera,
De Nederlandse Opera, and
The Los Angeles Music Center Opera Association
present

NIXON IN CHINA

Music by John Adams
Libretto by Alice Goodman
Co-commissioned by Houston Grand Opera,
The John F. Kennedy Center for the Performing Arts, and
Brooklyn Academy of Music

FIVE PERFORMANCES ONLY
MARCH 26 - APRIL 3, 1988
KENNEDY CENTER OPERA HOUSE
INSTANT-CHARGE   (202) 857-0900
Group Sales 634-7201   Information 254-3770

Above: Nixon in China, *co-produced by the Kennedy Center, made its debut in the Opera House in 1988.*

Top Right: *James Maddalena as Nixon departs from the plane in the opening scene of the opera.*

Houston Grand Opera and the Brooklyn Academy of Music, the Center commissioned John Adams's 1987 *Nixon in China*, staged by Peter Sellars, with choreography by Mark Morris and libretto by Alice Goodman—a remarkable convocation of talent. In fact, Goodman, Sellars, and Adams met together at the Center in 1985, where they worked intensively on the piece.

A new relationship between the Center and the Mariinsky Opera and Orchestra (formerly known as the Kirov Opera and Orchestra) blossomed in 2002, when a planned series of annual performances began with "A Tribute to Tchaikovsky," which included excerpts from several of the composer's operas. Other engagements in the partnership include *Eugene Onegin* (2003), *Turandot*, *Parsifal* (2006), *Falstaff* and *Il viaggio a Reims* (2007), *Otello*, and *The Queen of Spades* (2007). Prokofiev's *War and Peace*, which featured a 30-ton set and 331 Russian soloists, completed the agreement in 2010.

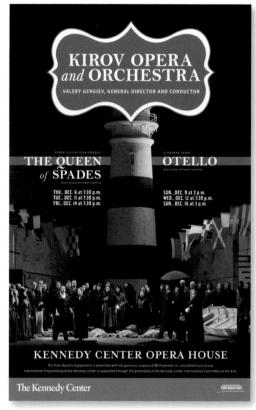

Left: *The Kirov Opera and Orchestra of Russia's Mariinsky Theatre performs a scene from Tchaikovsky's* The Queen of Spades.

Above: *2007 Kirov Opera poster for* The Queen of Spades *and* Otello

MARTIN FEINSTEIN

The Showman

Martin Feinstein, the Center's first Executive Director for Performing Arts, was recruited by Roger Stevens to manage programming and to bring leading performers to its stages. He also organized the first festivals. Feinstein was a mainstay of the Center from 1971 until 1979, when he left to become general director of the Washington Opera.

Feinstein fell in love with music as a twelve-year-old violinist in a Brooklyn settlement house orchestra. An interest in composing led him to begin following opera on the radio. One day, inspired by a broadcast from the Hippodrome in Manhattan, he went to the theater, using his school lunch money to buy a 35-cent ticket to see the Chicago Opera perform *Lucia di Lammermoor*. In succeeding weeks he returned for *Cavalleria Rusticana* and *Pagliacci*. His life was never the same.

Concluding that he lacked instrumental talent, young Feinstein quit the violin, but never gave up his passion for music. While in high school he sold librettos at the Metropolitan Opera House. Graduating in 1942 from City College of New York, where he majored in music and minored in journalism, he went on to Detroit's Wayne State University for a master's degree. He served in the U.S. Army in the Pacific on the staff of *Stars & Stripes* from 1943 until World War II ended.

Determined to work in the music world, Feinstein returned to New York, eventually persuading impresario Sol Hurok to hire him as assistant publicity director.

Feinstein's expertise and association with legendary impresario Sol Hurok enabled the Center to bring several companies of international repute to the United States for the first time, including the Bolshoi Ballet and Opera, the Berlin Opera, and many more.

Left: *Natalia Bessmertnova and Yuri Vladimirov in the Bolshoi's* Ivan the Terrible *in 1975.*

He rose to become vice president of Hurok Concerts. During those years Feinstein called himself a "press agent." However, he became expert not only at stirring publicity but also at the contractual, logistical, and aesthetic details of arts promotion and presentation on a worldwide basis.

Those experiences proved invaluable in the Center's formative years, when in addition filling an increasingly more complex performance calendar Feinstein used his international contacts to arrange with governments and institutions to subsidize appearances by their nations' leading artists and companies. Many relationships that he established continue to enrich the Center's programming.

Feinstein's countless coups included booking La Scala of Milan (the only time that opera company has been seen outside of Italy), the Berlin Opera, the Paris Opera, the Bolshoi Ballet, the Vienna Opera, the Royal Ballet, the Stuttgart Ballet, the first appearance of the Cuban Ballet since Castro took power, and others. Among many other important but less spectacular achievements, he renegotiated the Center's contracts with the stagehands and musicians unions into more equitable form. He introduced surtitles for operas, an innovation that became very popular. His favorite activity was conducting the annual "Hallelujah" chorus singalong, a task for which he strenuously rehearsed in his office before a few trusted colleagues expected to offer unvarnished but loving critiques.

The Berlin Opera's Lohengrin *during the Center's 1975–76 season.*

125

PLÁCIDO DOMINGO

Domingo pauses in thought during a rehearsal break in 2004. He maintains a packed schedule, and his activities are not limited to the Opera House; he has conducted several concerts in the Concert Hall as well.

Plácido Domingo, dubbed "the greatest tenor of all times" by BBC Music Magazine, has enjoyed a long association with the Center. Known for his strong, expressive tenor and his work as an administrator, Domingo received a Kennedy Center Honor in 2000. Throughout his career, he has had a tremendous impact and influence around the world and in particular in our nation's capital, where he led Washington National Opera from 1996 to 2011.

Domingo's prodigious abilities and appetite for work have lead to a dizzying array of achievements. In the fifty years since his debut in Verdi's *La Traviata* in 1961 with Mexico National Opera, he has sung at least 134 roles in more than 3,500 performances around the world and conducted more than 450 opera and symphony orchestra performances. He has won 12 Grammys and 2 Emmys, recorded 100 complete operas, and made 50 music videos.

Domingo's world-renowned career is marked by achievements not only in opera repertory and premieres of new works but by fresh, innovative ventures dedicated to bringing awareness of opera to a wider audience. With his fellow artists José Carreras and Luciano Pavarotti, Domingo created The Three Tenors, performing to sold-out audiences around the world. He has partnered with friends in both the pop and classical genres including John Denver, Dionne Warwick, Michael Bolton, Tony Bennett and many others, and through appearances on popular programs such as "Sesame Street" and "The Simpsons," Domingo and the art of opera are known to millions worldwide.

Domingo's association with the Center dates to March 6, 1972, when as a Founding Artist at the Center he first appeared onstage in a joint performance with Martina Arroyo in the Concert Hall. Almost exactly eleven years later, when the time came to renovate the Opera House, he returned to give another concert, directed by Julius Rudel, on March 7, 1983, to benefit the renovation effort. When the Metropolitan Opera came to the Center the following year, in April 1984, Domingo sang in the Met productions of Francesca da Rimini and Tosca. A high point came on November 15, 1986, when the Center and The Washington Opera co-produced the world premiere of Gian Carlo Menotti's Goya, starring Domingo in the title role.

In 1996, Domingo became Artistic Director of the company then known as The Washington Opera, which has performed in residence at the Center since its opening in 1971. Simply the presence of this renowned impresario attracted tremendous attention to the Washington opera scene, and under his guidance the respected regional company stepped into the international spotlight. Domingo is widely credited for taking the Opera to the next level, setting an ambitious artistic agenda that featured some of the world's most renowned singers and directors; programming of exciting new productions; the expansion of the company's national and international presence through radio and television broadcasts and touring; and increasing the company's commitment to its community through outreach and education programs.

Domingo curated fifteen seasons of opera in Washington, primarily at Center venues including the Eisenhower Theater, the Concert Hall, Millennium Stage and the Opera House. Hallmarks of his tenure include the establishment of the Domingo-Cafritz Young Artist Program, a prestigious training program for professional singers on the verge of international careers.

In 2003, Domingo became General Director, taking on additional administrative oversight, and in 2004, the company officially changed its name to Washington National Opera in recognition of the Congressional designation that Domingo helped to secure.

Domingo's tenure with Washington National Opera concluded in July 2011 but his legacy with the Company and the Kennedy Center lives on. He conducted the opening production of *Tosca* for the Company in September 2011, and the Domingo-Cafritz Young Artist program continues to train the up-and-coming opera stars of the next generation.

Domingo, with Victoria Vergara, stars in the world premiere of Menotti's Goya with the Washington National Opera in 1986.

The 2005 Festival of China included Tornado: Project for the Festival of China, artist Cai Guo Qiang's spectacular fireworks display over the Potomac River, featuring the first shells ever designed to simulate a tornado. They created a fantastic 500-foot-tall spiraling effect.

V. A FESTIVAL OF FESTIVALS

The Kennedy Center has always been an innovator and leader in the field of festivals for the arts. Over four decades the Center has used festivals to celebrate some of the more vibrant and fascinating aspects of music, dance, and theater. One of the more celebrated personalities in the Center's history, Marta Istomin, enhanced her legacy through her development of festivals at the Center.

Martin Feinstein, who always wanted to run an operation of his own, left the Center to manage the Washington Opera in 1979. As a replacement, Roger Stevens hired Marta Istomin as Artistic Director. Istomin had earned her arts management stripes working with her late husband, Pablo Casals, on festivals, a symphony orchestra, and a conservatory that the master cellist founded.

Extrapolating on Martin Feinstein's successful holiday fests, Istomin began presenting festivals during the summer. The original point was to enliven the summer, historically a less busy season, and what better way than with a free, themed, multiday event?

Initially, summer festivals focused on particular composers or genres of music, but gradually they came to cover dance and other disciplines, even

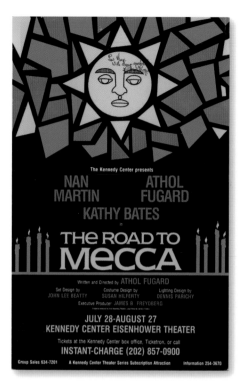

Above: Several of South African play-wright Athol Fugard's works have been produced at the Center: The Road to Mecca was presented in 1990, while in 1998, the world premiere of his work The Captain's Tiger was part of the African Odyssey festival.

Right: A dancer poses in Sasanka, a work commissioned by the Center and Dance Theatre of Harlem from South African choreographer Vincent Mantsoe for the African Odyssey festival.

multiple disciplines. Over the years, the festival ethos spread into other seasons and evolved into far larger and more complex presentations.

One festival that was quite popular was the annual Open House, begun in 1984. Held each September, the Open House was a sort of Center birthday party that kicked off the fall with a tasting menu that sometimes alerted festivalgoers to what's on for the coming months and sometimes hewed to a theme. Each Open House was just that: an eclectic array of dance, theater, music, and art that welcomes all comers. Originally, acts were chosen by audition; later online video served that purpose.

African Odyssey

Among the Center's most ambitious festivals was African Odyssey, a four-year program that began in 1997. Through 2000, the Center presented the full spectrum of African creativity: dance, theater, film, music, literature, photography, sculpture, textiles, clothing, food, and other touchstones of culture. Participating artists came from forty-four African countries, as well as from nations of the African diaspora in Central and South America and the Caribbean.

Each year of the festival pursued a theme. In 1997, a visual hallmark was the installation of stone sculptures from Zimbabwe and a dynamic array of textiles. The 1998 program included *The Captain's Tiger*, a new play by South Africa's Athol Fugard; a production of *Mother Courage and Her Children* by the National Theatre of Uganda; and the Africa Fête Tour, featuring popular musicians Salif Keita, Papa Wemba, Cheikh Lo, and Maryam Mursal. During 1999, the festival explored the pronounced artistic influence that Africa exerted on the New World as a result of slavery, particularly the cross-pollination of African and Latin music.

The Center commissioned new works for the festival. South African choreographer Vincent Mantsoe created *Sansanka* for Dance Theatre of Harlem. The Harlem dance company also performed the commission *South African Suite* with the Soweto String Quartet. Handspring Puppet Company of South Africa and Sogolon Puppet Company of Mali collaborated on the world premiere of *Zarafa*, a play based on the true story of one of the first giraffes to be brought to Europe. The Washington Ballet performed *Savannah*, by South African choreographer Boyzie Cekwana, and director-choreographer George Faison presented the musical theater piece *Queen Amina*, about a legendary African ruler.

Signal performances included the opening night Washington premiere of *African Portraits*, by trumpeter-composer Hannibal (Peterson), performed with the National Symphony Orchestra and the Morgan State University Choir;a Nigerian stage adaptation of Chinua Achebe's highly regarded novel *Things Fall Apart*; and appearances by trumpeter Hugh Masakela and singer Harry Belafonte, known for their work on behalf of human rights. Masakela also headlined African Odyssey Tour 2000, a two-month string of concerts across the United States by festival participants. Millennium Stage presented many of these performers. Education Department workshops and master classes across the Washington area brought local students and adults into contact with dance and theater companies and individual artists from Africa. The festival ended in 2000 with a Grand Foyer event directed by George Faison that drew more than seven thousand people for an evening of appearances by performers from Morocco, Tunisia, Nigeria, Kenya, and Benin.

Daily Dose

Millennium Stage isn't confined to a single area or enterprise, and is remarkably fluid and diverse. While it can be part of a grand expo like the African Odyssey, it can also be part of something more intimate and even spontaneous.

The most visible part of Performing Arts for Everyone occurs at 6 p.m. every day of the year. That's the hour at which Millennium Stage presents free live shows of every stripe, usually but not always at either end of the Great Foyer.

Millennium Stage had antecedents. For years, the Center presented, at no charge, occasional Grand Foyer Concerts. Acts played on the carpet, with limited publicity—a surprise dividend for ticket holders. Chairman James A. Johnson thought a more conventional approach would generate an audience of its own. He and President Larry Wilker reasoned that scheduling and promoting daily performances of a quality on par with that of main-stage offerings—for free—would create a varied and democratizing "destination event" that might reframe the Center in the American consciousness. Their

The line for free tickets for the Kennedy Center's production of The Twelve Days of Christmas., *an early free concert at the Center.*

gesture went a little further than anticipated. At the press conference announcing Millennium Stage, Johnson declared that it would run every day. Wilker was taken aback.

"We're closed Christmas!" the president stage-whispered.

"Not anymore!" the chairman replied.

The first show, featuring the Billy Taylor Trio, the Charlie Byrd Trio, and the John Adams Elementary School Orff Ensemble, took place at the south end of the Foyer. The crowd of a few hundred was encouraging—one down, 364 to go.

A few congested evenings made clear that toggling Millennium Stage performances between the north and south ends of the Great Foyer would

Three double-dutch jump-ropers from the Greenbelt S.I.T.Y Stars entertain an audience at the 2009 Open House.

Offbeat pop stars They Might Be Giants perform on the Millennium Stage.

allow schedulers to work around the Eisenhower Theater and Concert Hall curtain times and avoid human traffic jams. A second stage went up, with the Swedish chandeliers at either end of the Foyer removed to make room (the other chandeliers were raised to improve sight lines).

Summer 1997 showed how things could go. The African Odyssey festival was bringing a four-year parade of performers. Many were new to the United States and not likely to get commercial bookings during their visits. However, they would be a natural fit for Millennium Stage and its emphasis on diversity, quality, and cultural outreach. Other acts came by way of local auditions such as those used for Open Houses, until it was obvious that the relentless schedule demanded outside talent scouts. Prime among these were

A little girl shows off her dance moves during the 2005 Open House Arts Festival. Both Open House and Millennium Stage performances bring the arts into everyday life and give the Center tremendous outreach.

embassies, whose cultural attachés have access to world-class performers along with funds to cover travel costs.

The program found allies in Washington-area arts organizations already putting on shows at no charge

and happy to welcome another outlet. The Library of Congress partnered on the "Homegrown: Music of America" series. When they were in the capital for the National Folk Life Festival, artists engaged by the Smithsonian Institution were pleased to add bookings along the Potomac. While the National Museum of the American Indian was being built, its management sent performers from around the country to appear on Millennium Stage. Word went out to musicians and other talent with gigs in the metropolitan area, as well as to agents, managers and record companies, that Millennium Stage was the place to be—in effect, an eighth stage at the Center, but one that operated more like a club open seven nights a week.

The average Millennium Stage show draws more than four hundred people, but audiences can balloon. Roberta Flack has filled the Foyer, as have Juanes, They Might Be Giants, and other performers. In addition, promising artists such as Norah Jones and Ludacris appeared on Millennium Stage well before they became stars. To ensure that all attending can see and hear, the crew is ready with delay speakers, video displays, and sound equipment on the Terrace.

Productions have grown more complex. Once the typical act, a jazz trio, for example, played an hour, setting up and breaking down in a blink; now the stage

The Peking Opera brought their splendid 2005 production of Female Generals of the Yang Family, *part of the Festival of China.*

may host a seventeen-piece group, complete with bandstands, or be occupied by a dance troupe debuting a work that Millennium Stage commissioned and requiring intricate planning and execution.

In 1999, Millennium Stage embraced the live webcast. The first time out, Washington jazzman Marcus Johnson and group played before a single camera, with the performance sent out across the Internet and recorded for posterity. Dial-up was the order of the day, so transmission was slow and stuttering, but it succeeded. Webcasts evolved into a sophisticated four-camera switched shoot and seamless streaming. Shows were archived, allowing artists to link the recordings to their own sites and post or e-mail them—the ultimate audition tape. The webcasts are seen by viewers all over the world.

Every other year, in February and May, the Conservatory Project collaborates with leading American music schools to present the nation's best young artists in classical, jazz, musical theater, opera, and other musical disciplines. Using the Millennium Stage as a showcase, the project offers an advance look at tomorrow's talent.

Millennium Stage has become a complement to the Center at large that sometimes uses the Center, as in 2010's Gospel Music Festival. The congregation is central to this American musical form, so a community sing was organized. The program traced the African-American hymn's history in sacred songs, each performed by a

choir and preacher recruited from as far away as Massachusetts. An anchor choir stood by the John F. Kennedy bust, with a band at the Opera House entry and more than twenty singing groups and two thousand individuals arrayed around the foyer. As each hymn came up a different community came to the fore, backed by all the others. It was another rewarding and innovative experience—the Millennium Stage hallmark.

A Look to the East

In 2005, the Festival of China set a powerful precedent of breadth and complexity with a month-long exploration of that nation's arts and culture. Nearly nine hundred performers from China and the United States gave performances that ranged far and wide, including traditional and contemporary dance, symphonic and folkloric music, opera, ballet, acrobatics, and the visual arts. Orchestras and dance troupes from around China presented classical and

A young boy plays the drums during the Festival of China.

The Al-Farah Choir, known in Arabic as Joquat al-Farah, the Choir of Joy, performs at the 2009 Arabesque Festival. The Choir was founded at Our Lady of Damascus church in Damascus, Syria, in 1977 by Father Elias Zehlawi.

contemporary works. Academy Award-winning artist Tim Yip contributed *China Red*, a pair of outsized paper cut-outs (a traditional Chinese art form) attached to the glass panels separating the Hall of Nations and Hall of States from the Grand Foyer. Exhibits included statuary from Emperor Qin's tomb, photographs of Beijing, contemporary Chinese sculpture, and fashion by Vivienne Tam, Han Feng, Jeffrey Chow, Derek Lam, and other Chinese and Chinese émigré designers.

Going International

The Center's engagement on an international level, which had grown over the decades, entered a new phase in 2003 when Secretary of State Colin Powell invited Michael Kaiser to work in Mexico with managers of small arts organizations. In that country, government historically has provided 90 percent of arts funding, mostly to a few large entities. For three years, Kaiser worked with a group of thirty-five arts managers from around Mexico.

Subsequently, Kaiser and the Center developed arts management programs in China, Pakistan, and Palestine.

Welcome

There really is no place like the Kennedy Center. For one thing, it's a national monument, and you're always kind of aware of that. When you walk up the hill to the stage door you get a sense of scale and grandeur and importance. You know there are three enormous theaters in there with something going on or something being prepared for a performance, whether it's the National Symphony, an epic new production of a classic American play or an adventurous musical or some legendary international company of artists performing for free. It really does feel like our national crucible for the arts. It also has the distinction of being in the nation's capital, and the audiences reflect that—they're well educated and informed and experienced, so they're very discerning.

—Michael Cerveris

MICHAEL CERVERIS portrayed Giorgio in *Passion* during the Sondheim Celebration, sang the composer's songs with the National Symphony Orchestra, and has played Millennium Stage with his rock band, Cerveris.

A groundbreaking 2007 workshop in Cairo assembled one hundred forty arts leaders from seventeen Arab countries for two days of sessions with Kaiser. During 2008, he led symposia for arts managers in Central Europe, South America, and South Africa. His core message is that no matter what the specifics may be, arts managers who want to succeed must create strong, vibrant programs, that funding takes time, that planning is critical, and that to build audiences and donor bases, arts organizations need strong institutional identities. "Our focus has been on countries in transition, because I

Somali-born hip hop superstar K'naan attracted huge crowds when he played the Millennium Stage at the Arabesque Festival in February 2009. His songs fuse conscious calls for peaceful protest with Bob Marley-esque reggae touches.

South Africa helped many people cope with their anger while also producing change."

Exploring the Arab World

With Arabesque: Arts of the Arab World, the Center dramatically expanded its model for festivals. The three-week celebration, in February and March 2009, presented theater, dance, music, design, fashion, film, literature, and food from twenty-two Arab countries. The roster of some eight hundred performers included not only well-known figures but also artists making their U.S. and international debuts.

In addition to its stages, many unexpected parts of the Center's interior and other locations around Washington saw use in the festival for performances and exhibits. For instance, a display of wedding dresses, ranging from traditional to contemporary, lined the Hall of Nations and Hall of States, and became a favorite gathering place for visitors seeking a taste of home. A look at Arab cuisine brought visitors to several nations' embassies and official residences.

believe that the arts play an especially important part in troubled societies," Kaiser has said. "I believe the arts have the power to heal. Expressing anger, pain, and fear on stage is productive and effective. The protest theater of

Theater presentations included a *Richard III* that Kuwaiti writer-director Sulayman Al-Bassam placed in an Arab context, using a cast from across the Arab world. In *Alive from Palestine*, actors from the region under the direction of George Ibrahim told stories of ordinary life amid conflict. *Khamsoun*, written by Jalila Bakar and directed by Fadhil Jaibi, chronicled the half-century of changes in Tunisia since that nation gained independence. These and other performances occurred in Arabic, with English supertitles.

The festival's dance component was broad and diverse. In a world premiere, the Eisenhower Theater hosted *OMAN . . . O Man!,* a performance for young audiences choreographed by Emmy winner Debbie Allen and bringing together young Omani performers with American counterparts to dance to compositions by Arturo Sandoval. Classical Arabic music and dance were

The popular Brides of the Arab World exhibit was displayed throughout the Arabesque Festival in the Hall of Nations and Hall of States.

Young Omani performers collaborate with their American peers in the world premiere of choreographer Debbie Allen's OMAN... O Man!, a ground breaking dance driven extravaganza.

represented by Ensemble Al-Kindi with Sheikh Habboush and the Whirling Dervishes of Aleppo, Syria. The festival presented the U.S. premiere of *The Smala B. B.* by contemporary Moroccan choreographer Khalid Benghrib's Cie2k_far Dance Company and the Washington premiere of *D'ORIENT*, a contemporary dance paying homage to Arabic civilization created by Belgian dancer-choreographer Thierry Smits for Compagnie Thor.

Musically, the Arab world is very diverse, and the festival explored that variety. One concert presented singer Farida Mohammed Ali, backed by the Iraqi Maqam Ensemble, along with Moorish music from the Sahara by Mauretanian vocalist and instrumentalist Malouma. Vocalist, composer, and virtuoso violinist Simon Shaheen, accompanied by an orchestra, performed songs from the era of the 1920s through the 1950s, the golden age of Arab music.

The festival's literary series assembled a gathering of outstanding Arab writers to read and discuss original poetry and prose and to talk about such topics as gender in Arab literature, the impact of migration and exile on identity, Shakespeare in the Arab world, and expatriate Arab literature. Participants came from many of the twenty-two nations represented in the festival.

In addition to the popular costume display Brides of the Arab World, festival exhibits included Lebanese artist Lara Baladi's Roba Vecchia, an installation evoking the streets of Cairo. The Exploratorium, a multimedia display incorporating a specially commissioned 3-D film, explored Arab contributions in mathematics, medicine, astronomy, and chemistry between the eighth and fifteenth centuries. Other exhibits focused on calligraphy, jewelry, painting, and photography. A film festival within the festival offered half a dozen examples of Arab cinema.

As previous festivals had, Arabesque examined the importance of food in culture. A Taste of the Arab World

Pushing Forward

It's always an honor to be at the Kennedy Center. As America's premiere international performing arts space, the Center produces quality work in music, dance, and theater arts that reflects our diversity. The Center offers a platform for all our multicultural voices, presenting works true to the value of tradition yet also on the cutting edge, pushing all the performing arts forward.

—Debbie Allen

DEBBIE ALLEN, an award-winning producer, choreographer, and actress, has been a Kennedy Center Artist in Residence for more than ten years and served on the President's Committee for Arts and Humanities.

offered a discussion of a particular region's land, people, and culture, followed by a trip to an embassy and an ambassador's residence to taste featured countries' cuisines and explore their arts and cultures.

Under Kaiser, the Center's festivals deepened and broadened, focusing on countries (China, Japan, India), eras (the 1940s), genres (African-American choreography, a cappella music, gospel), individual artists such as William Shakespeare (but with a twist: performances took place at venues around Washington, engaging more than sixty local arts entities), and entire cultures (the Arab world). The Multicultural Children's Book Festival entered its second decade. The Tchaikovsky Festival brought together the National Symphony Orchestra and Leonard Slatkin with Yo-Yo Ma, Gil Shaham, and Yefim Bronfman, as well as the Kirov Opera and Ballet, The Suzanne Farrell Ballet, and the Vermeer String Quartet.

The International Ballet Festival featured six major companies presenting works spanning the range of classical ballet. The Prelude Festival debuted, an innovative annual event combining an introduction to the coming season and highlights of the entire Washington arts scene, further binding the Center to the city.

A young reader admires a book during the 11th annual Multicultural Children's Book Festival in 2006.

Above: *The 2008 Japan! Culture + Hyperculture festival included more than 450 artists, more than 40 performances, and more than a dozen free events, as well as Toyota's astonishing trumpet-playing robot.*

Upper Right: *Fireworks brighten the dark sky for the crowd at the Celebrate Mexico festival, honoring the 200-year anniversary of Mexico's independence and the 100-year anniversary of the Mexican Revolution.*

Right: *Children wave Mexican flags during the outdoor Fiesta Mexicana portion of the Celebrate Mexico festival.*

Musicians from the deserts of Rajasthan on an elaborate multilevel set perform Manganiyar Seduction, *directed by Roysten Abel, during the Maximum INDIA Festival.*

Classically trained Indian dancers Alarmel Valli and Madhavi Mudgal perform Samanvaya: A Coming Together *during the Kennedy Center's 2011 Maximum INDIA Festival.*

Principal musicians from the National Symphony Orchestra perform in the 2007 Teddy Bear Concert: More Tunes 'n' (Pig) Tales.

VI. EDUCATION AND THE ARTS

The American College Theater Festival has been associated with the Center since 1968, before the building even opened.

Embracing the arts is not simply about an interest in entertainment. The arts are also a living, moving history. The arts inspire. The arts touch on politics, science, philosophy, and cultural anthropology. The arts can elevate culture, can communicate concepts, can strengthen and deepen the ties connecting people.

Participation in the arts can also teach important lessons and skills about dedication, about precision, about commitment, about passion. When one devotes hours every week to mastering an instrument or learning lines for a play, one is also deepening character, strengthening parts of one's personality that will bring benefits for years to come. The Kennedy Center has prized arts education highly throughout its history, developing a number of innovative programs both at the Center and around the nation.

The student and teacher are at the heart of the Kennedy Center's education programs. There's a proverb that states, "Give a man a fish, and he will eat for a day, but teach a man to fish, and he will eat for a lifetime." In a similar vein, to give a child a glimpse of the beauty of ballet or the poignancy of a drama is tremendously rewarding, but to help a teacher bring the arts into the classroom, to be able to educate children on the importance and the rewards of making the arts a part of their lives, is absolutely critical.

The Center's approach to education is a fluid one, finding what is effective, discovering what is needed, and proceeding from there. Rather than institute some kind of one-size-fits-all rubric, the Center's programs seek to identify where expertise might be needed and tailor educational programs to those needs.

The Center has focused on three major educational areas: performances for young people; career development for young artists; and teaching, learning, and partnership programs from prekindergarten through grade twelve. The programs that the Center develops are evaluated at their source of implementation. If they are successful, the programs are distributed more widely. The educational programs begin on a local level and expand from

there to the state, regional, and national levels. People from across the nation and around the world participate in Kennedy Center programs without having to leave their communities.

Taking the Arts to School

The Center is located within an hour's drive of sixteen public school systems, as well as charter and independent schools and parents schooling at home. Students and teachers are able to attend theater, music, dance, and opera performances at the Center. In addition to performances, the Center also offers a myriad of educational opportunities.

Education is central to the Center's mission. Even before its opening, the Center was offering educational services such as the Kennedy Center American College Theater Festival (KCACTF). Begun with just a few colleges and universities in 1968, KCACTF now works with more than nine hundred college and university theater departments across the United States. Programs for children and teens, which began in 1973, were expanded in 1993 to include the Kennedy Center Theater for Young Audiences on Tour. Development of new generations of arts lovers has been a priority of education programs at the Kennedy Center, leading to the commission and production of more than 110 new works for young audiences. Through its New Visions, New Voices program, the Center has provided a development opportunity for fifty-eight theater companies to try out new theater works for young people.

However, the creation of new works is really the end of the process, not the beginning. In order to instill a profound love of the arts in a young person, that appreciation for music, dance, and theater should begin on a more fundamental level. The heart of the education program is the work done with teachers, teaching artists, and school administrators.

The arts can be tremendously useful

Left: *The May 2010 Kennedy Center production of the Caldecott Award–winning children's book by Mo Willems,* Knuffle Bunny: A Cautionary Tale, *featured Michael John Casey (left) as Dad and Stephanie D'Abruzzo (right) as Trixie.*

Right: *The intimate 324-seat Family Theater replaced the former AFI Film Theatre and opened in 2005, as part of the Center's commitment to performing arts and education for all ages.*

Above: *A little girl participates in a class at the Center in 1997.*

Above Right: *Advanced high school dancers warm up at the barre in one of the Center's Exploring Ballet with Suzanne Farrell classes.*

in bringing a class together, now more than ever. Darrell Ayers, Vice President of Education at the Kennedy Center, noticed, when visiting a classroom, that half the students seemed disengaged. But once an arts activity began, the entire class came alive. The teacher explained that her classroom had twenty-two languages spoken. When lecturing, half the class needed to translate for the other half. But the arts brought the class together. One doesn't need to understand English to understand the beat a drum provides, or to see how drawing diverging lines can create perspective in a drawing. The arts can foster unity and help teach in a universal way.

More than just a local performing

arts center, the Kennedy Center strives to aid its counterparts. Through the Partners in Education program, formal partnerships with over one hundred arts organizations across the nation have provided opportunities to initiate or expand professional development offerings for teachers and teaching artists in local school districts. In 2010, more than twenty-six thousand teachers received instruction on using the arts more effectively in the classrooms. Through the Kennedy Center Alliance for Arts Education Network, unaffiliated, independent not-for-profits have worked at the state level to help ensure that the arts should be part of a complete education for every child.

Educational Expansion

The Education Department continued to grow and diversify. A number of programs were added or expanded in 1993. Under its aegis, former New York City Ballet principal ballerina Suzanne Farrell agreed to offer a free weekend of ballet instruction at the Center. The enthusiastic response led to more such events and then to annual summer workshops. That program, Exploring Ballet with Suzanne Farrell (which led to the creation of The Suzanne Farrell Ballet), attracts dancers from around the globe. On her travels to audition prospective students, Farrell has given workshops in Mexico, China, Japan, and elsewhere.

The National Symphony Orchestra Youth Fellowship program began with talented music students from the metropolitan area who studied with NSO musicians, attended master classes and performances, received private lessons, and participated in other activities. An outgrowth of the fellowship program, in 1993, was the NSO Summer Music Institute, which selects young people from around the country to study each year with the Orchestra. About seventy students, from age fifteen to twenty, participate in the Institute, which offers four weeks of private lessons, rehearsals, coaching by NSO members, classes, and lectures. In addition to lessons and training, the students give free Millennium Stage concerts.

In that same year, the Center began

A talented youngster stretches at the barre during a Dance Theatre of Harlem Saturday residency ballet class.

Education

The Broward Center for the Performing Arts has participated in the Kennedy Center's "Partners in Education Program" since 1993. With the guidance of the Kennedy Center, our partnership, which includes the Broward Center, the School Board of Broward County, and the Broward Cultural Division, has been able to provide many outstanding arts integration professional development opportunities to thousands of educators in Broward County, Florida. Through the years, the Kennedy Center has assisted our team by offering opportunities that have sparked the imagination, channeled creative energies, and challenged our teachers to think in new ways, providing powerful tools for teaching and learning in and outside of the classroom. Creativity and innovation continue to be critical success factors for advancement in today's global economy, and the skills that our students take away from learning through the arts are proven to help them succeed.

Our partnership has given us the opportunity to bring a true vision of Arts Integration to our community, the sixth largest school district in the United States, through the support, dedication and encouragement of the Kennedy Center's outstanding Education Department.

—Sharon Brooks

SHARON BROOKS is the Director of Education, Broward Center for the Performing Arts, Ft. Lauderdale, Florida.

An empty school bus awaits its passengers. Hundreds of buses bring children to Center programs, often from one of the sixteen public school systems within an hour's drive of the Center.

to work with Arthur Mitchell, founder and former artistic director of the Dance Theatre of Harlem, to provide local D.C. students the opportunity to study ballet. A residency program offered Saturday classes at the Center. From across the metropolitan area, eighty to one hundred students came to study with Mr. Mitchell and his dancer colleagues in each of the subsequent years.

Education and Technology

The Center was an early and enthusiastic adopter of new media in education. ARTSEDGE (www.artsedge.kennedy-center.org), an online presence launched in 1996, offers K–12 educators, students, individuals, and families access to digital tools to enhance arts education. It is telling that of the eleven million people who participate in Center educational programs each year, four million do so through this website. More people use the resources of ARTSEDGE daily than the total number of seats in every Center theater. The program reaches out to both traditional educators and

to out-of-school teachers and families schooling children at home with free digital resources. These include lesson plans, audio and video clips, and interactive online modules, all streamlined

Suzanne Farrell instructs dancers during a class, part of Exploring Ballet with Suzanne Farrell summer intensive.

Ambassador Jean Kennedy Smith and a small child admire artwork during the 2010 International VSA Festival. In 2011, Smith was awarded the Presidential Medal of Freedom for her work with VSA and the disabled.

for easier browsing and upgraded continually to reflect best practices in educational media and instructional programs using multiple media.

Through the website, students can learn about the dances associated with Chinese New Year or identify the music and artists connected to Harlem or discover the history of blues music. They can learn the beautiful language of ballet or discover how glass is used to create works of art.

The Internet is a valuable tool, but an important aspect of arts education is hands-on instruction. Any Given Child, a part of Center educational efforts since 2008, aims to guarantee systematic, meaningful arts education using an affordable model that combines the resources of a school district, local arts groups, and the Center. In the program, designed for grades K–8, Center staff members work with community leaders and school administrators to develop a long-range plan for arts education tailor-made for that school district. The team reviews existing arts resources in the school district and education programs offered by local arts organizations

and companies. Using that snapshot of arts education resources, a community-specific plan is developed. Rather than leave after helping with the creation of the plan, the Kennedy Center assists with the implementation, ensuring that arts are part of each child's education.

For all Kennedy Center education programs, the emphasis is on adapting its programs to the needs of individuals and local communities.

VSA

Arts education isn't only about teaching how to play musical instruments or how to paint. It's also about strengthening communities, and bringing the arts to people who might not otherwise have access to it. The Center reaches out to people living with disabilities through its affiliation with VSA, the international organization on arts and disability. This international nonprofit founded in 1974 by Ambassador Jean Kennedy Smith (and at one point called Very Special Arts before changing to simply VSA), works to ensure that people living with disabilities learn through the arts, participate in them and enjoy them.

Initially part of the Center, the organization struck off on its own, but in 2006 it returned to become a full Kennedy Center affiliate.

VSA often produces events at the Kennedy Center. The 2010 International VSA Festival drew more than two thousand participants from around the world to the Center and other Washington-area venues. The festival included *See What I'm Saying: The Deaf Entertainers Documentary*, performances by Salif Keita (known as the "Golden Voice of Africa"), *Ben X*, a film about a young man with Asperger's syndrome, Australia's indie rock sensation Rudely Interrupted, multi-instrumentalist Raul Midón, and the AXIS Dance Company.

VSA programs provide educators, parents, and artists with resources and tools to support arts programming in schools and communities. The VSA credo is that all young people living with disabilities deserve access to high quality arts learning; that artists in schools and art educators should be prepared to instruct students living with disabilities; that people of all ages with disabilities should have complete access to cultural facilities

Michael Kaiser is interviewed at the Nashville Children's Theatre in August 2009 as part of the Center's Arts in Crisis fifty-state tour. Kaiser visited all fifty states, D.C., and Puerto Rico to counsel arts leaders on maintaining fiscal and artistic stability during the economic downturn.

and activities; that individuals with living disabilities aspiring to careers in the arts should have the chance to develop appropriate skills; and that artists living with disabilities be given equal opportunities to display their talents as those without disabilities. Some of its signature programs include the International Young Soloists Competition and the Playwright's Discovery Program, where young people are encouraged to write plays that deal with a disability or a disability issue. Through its state and international network of affiliates, more than seven million people are engaged in VSA programs in the United States and in fifty-one countries around the world.

Professional Development

Education isn't only for children. Education can affect life at any age. The Council of Metropolitan Arts Supervisors and the Principals' Arts Education Forum each meet quarterly at the Center. These two initiatives offer area administrators forums in which to exchange ideas about arts education.

The Center also offers teachers and teaching artists opportunities for

Partnerships

I was fortunate enough to be among the founding teams of the Partners in Education program, from its very first year continuing on. The Partnership has been an absolutely vital part of our school/arts center/community program since first meeting.

The emphasis on teachers and their needs has been one of the most important aspects of the program. As a teacher-artist myself, I was most excited about the Kennedy Center's insistence that the workshops be presented to teachers who would then be able to pass the information and inspiration on to their own students. We were able to have both workshops with fabulous leaders like Sandy Lyne and Lenore Blank Kelnor and to feel like we could do just what they did ourselves. The organized, meticulously detailed, and very clear instructions in those workshops translated into dynamic and delightful arts experiences to be shared with students and others.

In addition to meeting these important workshop leaders and sometimes bringing them into our communities (as we did with both artists listed above), we were given the very important opportunity to network with other states' education and arts organizations who shared similar concerns and interests, an invaluable experience in and of itself. We have constantly drawn on both old and new partners in our day-to-day work in the trenches of the schools and the centers and to have that resource is a privilege not to be underestimated. The work of many kindred spirits lightens the load for all of us.

The Kennedy Center Arts Partnership team has done what a true leader should do: inform, include, and inspire.

—Jeanne Averill

JEANNE AVERILL is recognized nationally for her talents as a teacher as well as for her performances as an actress.

professional development. Through the Changing Education Through the Arts program, teachers study with their colleagues in courses and workshops led by expert teaching artists and arts educators. They learn about the arts and ways to integrate them in their teaching. After school, during the school day, on weekends, and during the summer, they participate in a range of programs designed to meet their varying needs, interests, and experiences. Each year, more than seven hundred local teachers participate in approximately sixty courses and workshops.

The Art of Arts Management

The desire to educate professionals in the intricacies of arts management led to the development of the DeVos Institute for Arts Management at the Kennedy Center.

Created to address gaps in professional development facing the arts, the Institute harnesses the deep, broad expertise available at the Center and elsewhere to train arts managers, non-profits, and board members. Institute programs offer practical guidance on strategic and artistic planning, board management, marketing, fund-raising, financial management, and technology. Michael Kaiser, who will be Center president until 2014, plans to segue into presiding full time over the Institute, funded since 2010 by the DeVos family of Grand Rapids, Michigan.

Since 2001, the Institute annually has enrolled as Fellows ten arts managers from around the world. Participants generally are several years into careers in arts management and wish to deepen their skills. They arrive in September and stay through May to study strategic planning, marketing, and development, and also participate in professional development seminars. Fellows rotate through three assignments with Center departments, gaining valuable practical experience.

Under the aegis of the Institute, the Capacity Building for Culturally Specific Arts Organizations program began to offer free training and technical support for African-American, Latino, Asian-American, and Native American arts organizations. The Capacity Building program arranges for senior staff members at the Center to offer training and technical support for executive, artistic, and board leadership of arts organizations at no charge. Since 2002, the program has worked with nearly three hundred institutions in New York City, seventy-four in the Washington, D.C., area, and thirty-six in the Midwest. Forty organizations dedicated to African-American, Latino, Asian-American, and Native American arts have participated, as have ten organizations in select U.S. cities developing next-generation arts spaces. Arts managers and leaders and governments in Argentina, China, the Czech Republic, Egypt, Israel, Mexico, the Palestinian Territories, Romania, and South Africa also have participated.

Each July since 2009, the International Fellowship Program has welcomed as many as twenty mid- to high-level arts leaders from nonprofit performing arts organizations abroad for an intensive full-time session lasting four weeks. To complete their course of study, International Fellows return annually for three consecutive summers to

Conductor Iván Fischer addresses the audience in a 2007 NSO education performance.

I Died at the Kennedy Center

In fall 2000, I was a third grader in University Park, Maryland. One of my older sisters had been studying for years at the Washington School of Ballet. Every Christmas, the school performed The Nutcracker at the Warner Theatre in Washington, D.C. This particular production had more roles for boys than it had boys to fill them, so the producers asked dancers if they had younger brothers interested in going onstage. My family encouraged me, and that December I made my ballet debut as a Little Chef.

I must have made an impression. The next May, the school's ballet master, Septime Webre, asked me to perform in a Washington Ballet production of Romeo and Juliet at the Kennedy Center. The role was a boy killed accidentally in a sword fight. I hesitated, but then Mr. Webre offered my sister a role as well. I still joke about getting Kaitlin her first paying job in dance.

My scene, which began the ballet, was chaotic. I had to learn when and where to stand to be in the right place at the right time for a duelist to shove a prop rapier between my right arm and ribcage. The dancer playing my "mother" was good about guiding me into position. Rehearsals were a blur, and I didn't understand very well what dying meant, but I did a pretty good job of going limp, creating the illusion that I'd been stabbed. After I collapsed, my distraught "father" would carry me offstage.

Opening night, I made my way through the crowd of extras and met with the duelist's blade. My stage father picked me up; I lay slack in his arms as he carried me into the wings. In the next day's paper, a reviewer wrote, "A few minutes into the ballet, a gleefully freewheeling sword-fighting scene ends with a child's death, a needless bit of shock value."

My sister went on to become a professional dancer. I quit show business while I was ahead.

—Thomas Madzelan

THOMAS MADZELAN is a student at Loyola University Chicago.

take classes and refine strategic plans for their organizations.

Every fall and spring, the Institute accepts interns interested in careers in arts management and arts education. The twenty or so undergraduate and graduate students and recent graduates picked for these twelve-week, full-time sessions obtain valuable experience and encounter meaningful learning opportunities as they move through assignments at Center offices. Working with a supervisor, each intern sets goals and completes a project. The schedule includes weekly seminars led by executives of the Center and other major area arts institutions. Participants keep portfolios and undergo evaluations. Space permitting, interns may attend Center performances, workshops, and classes at no charge.

In 2004, an annual Board Development Seminar was introduced to offer intensive training to current and prospective board members of arts organizations worldwide. Taught by Kaiser and other senior staff, the October sessions, which usually sell out, cover building institutional identity, strategic planning, fund-raising, not-for-profit financial analysis, marketing, hiring an executive director, and recruiting and managing boards.

The Arts in Crisis initiative, developed in 2009 in response to the economic downturn, aided nonprofit arts organizations coping with shrinking income and endowments. Arts in Crisis offered at no charge confidential counsel in fund-raising, board management, budgeting, marketing, and other pertinent areas. Volunteering their time and expertise, Center senior staff and senior arts managers nationwide served as mentors by e-mail, phone, and personal visits. Arts in Crisis connected 760 organizations with nearly 140 mentors. To infuse the program with real-world perspective, the Institute held town hall meetings in sixty-nine cities; Michael Kaiser himself visited all fifty states. These symposia, scheduled in partnership with local arts or civic bodies, involved some eleven thousand people discussing challenges to nonprofit arts groups such as board management, marketing, and fund-raising.

The Center also operates artsmanager.org, a website for current and future arts managers, board members, educators, and students. Arts managers can use the site to connect with peers worldwide, illuminating common challenges and offering advice. The site features case studies, a strategic planning guide, a resource center, a discussion board, blog posts by Kaiser, and a Q&A forum.

With the DeVos family's generosity underpinning the Institute's growth, David Rubenstein's election to the chairmanship of the board further solidifying Center leadership, and Michael Kaiser remaining as president of the Center until 2014, the Institute's path is secure, and the Center's role in educating future generations of arts managers assured, along with its place in the performing arts.

Clockwise from left: *Angela Basset, Lawrence Fishburne, Cicely Tyson, and Chita Rivera (Honoree) embrace at the 2002 Honors.*

VII. THE HONORS

Art can entertain. It can also inspire, provoke, compel, enlighten, and transform. Artists who reach the pinnacle of their profession can thrill audiences and also elevate their medium, employing it to create something profound. It only seems fitting that such titans be recognized. For those artists, the Kennedy Center Honors were created.

Begun in 1978, the Kennedy Center Honors have become one of the Center's best-known events. The annual proceedings acknowledge a handful of artists, chosen by the board of trustees, for lifetime achievements enriching American culture. More than 150 Honors medallions in dance, music, theater, opera, motion pictures, and television have been awarded. The ceremony takes place during an intimate dinner hosted by the Secretary of State at the State Department. The next night, after a reception at the White House, Honorees join the President and First Lady in the Presidential Box of the Opera House to receive accolades from peers and admirers. The program obeys what insiders call Cary Grant's Law, which stipulates that Honorees need do nothing but stand there—a touch that appealed to Grant, who prized his medallion and happily returned for years to read the citations at the State Department dinner.

The Honors had their genesis in the AFI's tenth anniversary celebration. An Opera House gala in 1977 honored the fifty greatest American films. The weekend, bright with Hollywood wattage, included a White House reception.

Afterward, AFI founder George Stevens Jr. thanked Roger Stevens for making the Opera House available. As they chatted, the younger man offhandedly said the Center ought to do something similar for all the arts.

After numerous performances at the Center, conductor and composer Leonard Bernstein has a quiet moment at the 1980 awards show, when he became an Honoree.

"Got any ideas?" the chairman said.

George Stevens returned the next day with a proposal. Roger Stevens liked it. The next year, George Stevens and the late Nick Vanoff produced the event. Stevens still produces it. Ever since Ronald Reagan took office, the Honors have been one of the highlights of the D.C. social season, and the CBS special featuring the gala has become a TV evergreen. Stevens and son Michael have won two Emmy Awards for the telecast, also recognized with a Peabody Award and citations from the Writers Guild of America.

The Honors recognize significant contributions to the arts but also speak volumes more. Sidney Poitier has always been an outstanding actor, but his success meant more than that. His film roles showed that an African-American actor, and character, could be smart, compassionate, capable, dignified, and strong. Director and producer Steven Spielberg has made billions of dollars for Hollywood, but his *Schindler's List* brought the reality of the Holocaust to generations too young to remember World War II, reminding a nation of the horrors of war, and the heroism a single flawed man might be capable of. Arthur Miller's *The Crucible* was a gripping drama, but it also helped to give a new perspective to the McCarthy witch hunts, a brave statement at a time when so many resigned themselves to terrified silence. Ray Charles created phenomenal music, but he also showed that a man who grew up poor, blind, and suffering from institutionalized racism could still rise to the top of the entertainment world through talent, hard work, and a commitment to excellence.

Top left: *Writer, producer, playwright, author, and founder of the American Film Institute, George Stevens, Jr. has produced or co-produced the Honors for more than 30 years.*

Middle left: *Broadcaster and commentator Walter Cronkite was the show's first host; he continued in that role until 2002.*

Lower left: *Honoree George Balanchine, President Jimmy Carter, and Mrs. Carter enjoy a performance at the 1978 Honors.*

THE KENNEDY CENTER HONOREES BY YEAR

2011 *(Thirty-fourth Year)*

Barbara Cook
Neil Diamond
Yo-Yo Ma
Sonny Rollins
Meryl Streep

2010 *(Thirty-third Year)*

Jerry Herman
Merle Haggard
Bill T. Jones
Paul McCartney
Oprah Winfrey

2009 *(Thirty-second Year)*

Mel Brooks
Dave Brubeck
Grace Bumbry
Robert De Niro
Bruce Springsteen

2008 *(Thirty-first Year)*

Roger Daltrey
Morgan Freeman
George Jones
Barbra Streisand
Twyla Tharp
Pete Townshend

2007 *(Thirtieth Year)*

Leon Fleisher
Steve Martin
Diana Ross
Martin Scorsese
Brian Wilson

2006 *(Twenty-ninth Year)*

Andrew Lloyd Webber
Zubin Mehta
Dolly Parton
William "Smokey" Robinson
Steven Spielberg

2005 *(Twenty-eighth Year)*

Tony Bennett
Suzanne Farrell
Julie Harris
Robert Redford
Tina Turner

2004 *(Twenty-seventh Year)*

Warren Beatty
Ossie Davis
Ruby Dee
Elton John
Joan Sutherland
John Williams

Top: The 2010 Honors Class included (clockwise from left) Merle Haggard, Bill T. Jones, Paul McCartney, Oprah Winfrey, and Jerry Herman.

Bottom: 2008 Honoree George Jones sits with President George W. Bush and Mrs. Bush.

Top: 2007 Honoree Diana Ross flashes a dazzling smile.

Bottom: 2006 Honorees Dolly Parton and Smokey Robinson share a laugh on the red carpet.

Left: *A star-studded audience fills the Opera House at the 1997 Kennedy Center Honors.*

Above: *Caroline Kennedy, daughter of President John F. Kennedy, hosts the 2008 Kennedy Center Honors. She has hosted the annual program since 2003.*

2003 (Twenty-sixth Year)

James Brown
Carol Burnett
Loretta Lynn
Mike Nichols
Itzhak Perlman

2002 (Twenty-fifth Year)

James Earl Jones
James Levine
Chita Rivera
Paul Simon
Elizabeth Taylor

2001 (Twenty-fourth Year)

Julie Andrews
Van Cliburn
Quincy Jones
Jack Nicholson
Luciano Pavarotti

2000 (Twenty-third Year)

Mikhail Baryshnikov
Chuck Berry
Plácido Domingo
Clint Eastwood
Angela Lansbury

Top: *2002 Honoree James Earl Jones stars in* Of Mice and Men *at the Center.*

Bottom: *2002 Honorees Paul Simon and Elizabeth Taylor shake hands.*

1999 (Twenty-second Year)

Victor Borge
Sean Connery
Judith Jamison
Jason Robards, Jr.
Stevie Wonder

1998 (Twenty-first Year)

Bill Cosby
John Kander
Fred Ebb
Willie Nelson
Andre Previn
Shirley Temple (Black)

1997 (Twentieth Year)

Lauren Bacall
Bob Dylan
Charlton Heston
Jessye Norman
Edward Villella

1996 (Nineteenth Year)

Edward Albee
Benny Carter
Johnny Cash
Jack Lemmon
Maria Tallchief

Top: *2000 Honoree Angela Lansbury appears in a production of* Sweeney Todd *at the Center in 1980.*

Bottom: *1997 Honoree Charlton Heston was onstage at the Center in* The Caine Mutiny Court-Martial.

1995 *(Eighteenth Year)*

Jacques d'Amboise
Marilyn Horne
Riley "B.B." King
Sidney Poitier
Neil Simon

1994 *(Seventeenth Year)*

Kirk Douglas
Aretha Franklin
Morton Gould
Harold Prince
Pete Seeger

1993 *(Sixteenth Year)*

Johnny Carson
Arthur Mitchell
Sir Georg Solti
Stephen Sondheim
Marion Williams

1992 *(Fifteenth Year)*

Lionel Hampton
Paul Newman

Joanne Woodward
Ginger Rogers
Mstislav Rostropovich
Paul Taylor

1991 *(Fourteenth Year)*

Roy Acuff
Betty Comden
Adolph Green
Fayard Nicholas
Harold Nicholas
Gregory Peck
Robert Shaw

1990 *(Thirteenth Year)*

Dizzy Gillespie
Katharine Hepburn
Risë Stevens
Jule Styne
Billy Wilder

1989 *(Twelfth Year)*

Harry Belafonte
Claudette Colbert

Alexandra Danilova
Mary Martin
William Schuman

1988 *(Eleventh Year)*

Alvin Ailey
George Burns
Myrna Loy
Alexander Schneider
Roger L. Stevens

1987 *(Tenth Year)*

Perry Como
Bette Davis
Sammy Davis, Jr.
Nathan Milstein
Alwin Nikolais

1986 *(Ninth Year)*

Lucille Ball
Ray Charles
Hume Cronyn
Jessica Tandy
Yehudi Menuhin
Antony Tudor

Top: *1983 Honorees Frank Sinatra (left) and Elia Kazan (right) share a moment.*

Bottom: *1983 Honoree James Stewart sits with President and Mrs. Reagan.*

Top: *1979 Honoree Henry Fonda in the 1977 world premier of* The First Monday in October *at the Center.*

Bottom: *1979 Honoree Martha Graham (right) with 1982 Honoree Lillian Gish (left)*

1985 *(Eighth Year)*

Merce Cunningham
Irene Dunne
Bob Hope
Alan Jay Lerner
Frederick Loewe
Beverly Sills

1984 *(Seventh Year)*

Lena Horne
Danny Kaye
Gian Carlo Menotti
Arthur Miller
Isaac Stern

1983 *(Sixth Year)*

Katherine Dunham
Elia Kazan
Frank Sinatra

James Stewart
Virgil Thomson

1982 *(Fifth Year)*

George Abbott
Lillian Gish
Benny Goodman
Gene Kelly
Eugene Ormandy

1981 *(Fourth Year)*

Count Basie
Cary Grant
Helen Hayes
Jerome Robbins
Rudolf Serkin

1980 *(Third Year)*

Leonard Bernstein
James Cagney

Agnes deMille
Lynn Fontanne
Leontyne Price

1979 *(Second Year)*

Aaron Copland
Ella Fitzgerald
Henry Fonda
Martha Graham
Tennessee Williams

1978 *(Inaugural Year)*

Marian Anderson
Fred Astaire
George Balanchine
Richard Rodgers
Arthur Rubinstein

These people, and many more, were unquestionably outstanding practitioners of their art, but they were also significant contributors to our culture.

President Bill Clinton conducts the National Symphony Orchestra at the reopening of the Kennedy Center Concert Hall in 1997 after its extensive renovation.

VIII. THE CENTER, THE CITY, THE NATION, THE WORLD

Theater banners, Belgian mirrors, Orrefors crystal chandeliers and the famous bronze bust of President Kennedy decorate the Center's Grand Foyer, which has welcomed thousands of visitors and performers from the metropolitan area, the United States, and the world.

The Center's first forty years did not pass without rancor. Skeptics decried the site's distance from downtown, its detachment from the city, and its location on the rackety Potomac flyway.

When Edward Durell Stone redid his design, critics jeered his "shining Kleenex box upon a hill." Naysayers warned that the Center would blind audiences to Washington's other creative offerings, that its enormous maw would gobble talent and ticket buyers needed elsewhere in town, that with the noblest of intentions government had introduced an invasive exotic entity likely to prosper at the expense of local art.

There were snags, literal and figurative. One night in the 1970s a curtain rose on the American Ballet Theatre, then caught, spilling weights that held the drape straight. The cast might as well have been trying to perform on ice. When the third dancer came down, so did the curtain, to mask a hurried cleanup.

Still, the place acquired admirers of all sorts. Some did come for the status display, others out of pure love for art, for star-powered showbiz sizzle, for a cool breath in hot summer, for the fleeting splendor of Farrell mid-leap or Rostropovich mid-fingerboard or Domingo mid-aria, magic-hour light pouring through sixty-foot clerestories along a blimp-worthy foyer. They came for Tuba Christmases, Open Houses, festivals and their creative clamor, the riotous *Noises Off*, the shattering moment in *Sweeney Todd* when the demon barber's blade must fall in the worst way possible, the startling maturation the second time around of *Ragtime* from production to phenomenon to Broadway. They came simply to stand in the halls and look, and, looking, enjoy.

Warnings that the Center would harm Washington's arts scene were not just wrong, but dramatically so. Where the capital once had a handful of theater companies, there now are scores. In the decades since the Center opened more than a dozen local and regional arts centers have come into being around the metropolitan area, at least nine of them since 2000.

The Center's abundant arts programs offer much for all.

Lower left: *A young family laughs at a 2009 Open House performance.*

Lower right: *An enthusiastic crowd dances at a performance by Cajun band Feufollet at the 2005 Open House Arts Festival.*

A performance of the annual Merry Tuba Christmas! led by Harvey Phillips, on the Millennium Stage, welcomes hundreds of exuberant tuba players.

Left: *Assistant principal violinist William Foster practices with a student during the NSO's North Dakota Residency in 2003. The Center's outreach programs extend throughout the nation.*

Below: *Alexandra Silber (left) and Tyne Daly (right) at the first rehearsal for the 2010 production of Terrence McNally's Master Class at the Center.*

Educational programs solidified the Center's ties to Washington, D.C., and environs through concrete activities that benefited students in the city and the suburbs. Programs such as the Kennedy Center American College Theater Festival, ballet workshops, and training brought young performers and arts managers to the Center and took the Center's name nationwide and international.

The National Symphony Orchestra, through its American Residency program, brought classical music to overlooked areas of the country.

Festivals at the Center matured into an ongoing effort to illuminate genres and cultures. These activities reached far and wide across the country, and gradually around the world, and the country and the world reached back.

As an educator, the Center has developed broadly and deeply. The emergence of the DeVos Institute for Arts Management at the Kennedy Center bespeaks a seriousness of purpose, an intention to stay on for the long haul as a presence in this critical arena, and the recognition that an important aspect of art needs advocates who are well schooled in skills of crucial importance.

As a performing space, the Center, thanks to its official status and its sheer size, had automatic pride of place. But pride of place doesn't guarantee public acceptance and affection. Those must be earned, and the Center earned them. How? Surely one factor was a myriad of presentations of all types; from high art to low, from tragedy to comedy, from grand and eloquent stagings to bare-bones, black-box shows.

Availability matters here, as do flexibility and versatility. It all boils down to being there and being ready with something that people might not have known they wanted, but recognized instantly, and embraced. That embrace wasn't a one-night stand, but a forty-year love affair that grew and deepened

and changed those who have been partners to it.

One gauge of popular affection is the Friends of the Kennedy Center. Since its founding in 1965, the group has enlisted and trained thousands of energetic volunteers. Some years the five hundred

Mrs. Reagan celebrates her birthday backstage with President Reagan and the cast of Les Misérables *in 1988.*

Left: *Bernadette Peters performs at a special Center celebration of Senator Edward Kennedy's 77th birthday in 2009.*

Above: *Senator Kennedy applauds with Mrs. Obama (left), Senator John Kerry, and Victoria Reggie Kennedy (right) at his birthday celebration.*

or so members log more than eighty thousand collective hours of service. On the job eleven hours a day, every day, Friends perform thousands of vital tasks ranging from data processing to selling T-shirts. They generate actual millions by staffing the gift shops and have contributed millions more in personal donations. Arts organizations worldwide look to the Friends as a model for their volunteer programs. And just as programming and policies at the Center have come to reflect American diversity, the Friends have evolved from a group of ladies of a certain age and shade to the full range of colors, ages, and genders,

President Obama, who led a chorus of "Happy Birthday" during Senator Kennedy's birthday celebration, waves from the stage. Other celebrants onstage include Bill Cosby, Denyce Graves, and James Taylor.

all the while offering their hard work and their helpful smiles.

Through the efforts of the Friends, the board, and the staff, the Kennedy Center became a Washington place, and an American place, and a place the world knows. The National Symphony Orchestra and the Washington National Opera went from tenant to integral element. Programs developed to enrich arts education in the schools of the capital and environs. Shrubs grew in. Roofs got fixed. The Center was not eclipsing but encouraging, not overshadowing but empowering. Audiences saw this, and responded with an enthusiasm that shows no signs of ending. The longer the Center is around, the more people grow to value it.

That evolution didn't stop at the Potomac's edge, or at the Beltway, or at the border. From the start, millions of visitors to Washington added the Center to their capital itineraries, and whether they saw a performance or simply stretched their legs, they spread the word about the unparalleled experience of walking the halls and Foyer, of standing on the terraces low and high.

The Center thrived. Americans identified with it, and people elsewhere identified it with America. That identification results from the Center's history, whose theme is a constant testing of ideas. Very different people have run the institution in very different ways, but through each stage the Center has continued to evolve. In its forty-year arc, the John F. Kennedy Center for the Performing Arts has come through wildly differing times and swings in American life, embracing and transcending those differences and variations, never retracing its steps but always growing, always moving forward, always trying something new.

AUTHOR'S NOTE

Michael Dolan would like to thank Alicia Adams, Darrell Ayers, Brooks Boeke, Robert Barnett, Bill Becker, Mickey Berra, Bret Burzio, Scott Bushnell, Tiki Davies, Claudette Donlon, John Dow, Suzanne Farrell, Henry Fogel, Edwin Fontánez, Mary Jo Ford, Nancy Gasper, Alma Gildenhorn, Judy Gruber, Mariellen Grutz, Jessica Happel, Michael Hackshaw, Steve Hawkins, Amanda Hunter, Marta Istomin, James Johnson, Michael Kaiser, Joseph Kalichstein, Kathleen Kelly, Richard Kidwell, David Kitto, Barry Konig, Emily Krahn, Ben Loehnen, Alan Levine, Dan Madzelan, Kaitlin Madzelan, Jane Martin, Dorothy and Bill McSweeny, Bob Moriarty, Liza Mundy, Chuck Naylor, Patricia O'Kelly, Chris O'Toole, Priscilla Painton, Michelle Pendoley, Steve Pohl, Alma Johnson Powell, Brian Powers, Charles Reinhart, Garth Ross, David Rubenstein, Joe Savia, Rich Schneider, Sheldon Schwartz, Ellen Scordato, Jack Shafer, Rosa Shaw, Leonard Silverstein, Nola Solomon, George Stevens, Jr., Kevin Struthers, Colby Thornton, Jamie van der Vink, the fabulous Warren boys, Larry Wilker, Max Woodward, and all who took the trouble to speak about the place where they and so many others have strutted their hour, fretful or not, upon the Kennedy Center stage. Mr. Dolan would like to note: "I owe much to Ted Libbey's The National Symphony Orchestra and to Richard Freed's liner notes for the CD set National Symphony Orchestra, Seventy-Fifth Anniversary 1931–2006. And, of course, thank you Eileen for everything."

ABOUT THE AUTHORS

MICHAEL DOLAN is the author of *The American Porch: An Informal History of an Informal Place* and the play *Desert One* and coeditor of E*cho Ever Proudly: Gonzaga College High School in the Press 1821–1899*. He has written for the *New Yorker, Slate, Outside*, the *New York Times*, and many other publications and has written and produced scores of TV documentaries. A bassist-songwriter and cofounder of the bands The Sherier Mountain Boys and WMD, he lives in Washington, D.C., three miles upriver from the Kennedy Center.

MICHAEL SHOHL is a writer and editor who lives in New York City.

BIBLIOGRAPHY

Becker, Ralph E. *Miracle on the Potomac: The Kennedy Center from the Beginning*. Silver Spring, MD: Bartleby, 1990.

Doráti, Antal. *Notes of Seven Decades*. London: Hodder & Stoughton, 1979.

"Former National Park Service System Units: An Analysis," last modified January 16, 2003. http://www.nps.gov/history/history/hisnps/npshistory/formerparks.htm.

Gill, Brendan. *John F. Kennedy Center for the Performing Arts*. New York: Abrams, 1981.

——"Welcoming the Muses," *New Yorker*, September 26, 1981.

Halberstam, David. *The Fifties*. New York: Villard, 1993.

Kaiser, Michael M. *The Art of the Turnaround: Creating and Maintaining Healthy Arts Organizations*. Boston: Brandeis, 2008.

Kaiser, Michael M. *Leading Roles: 50 Questions Every Arts Board Should Ask*. Boston: Brandeis, 2010.

Kennedy Center website. http://www.kennedy-center.org.

"Opening Night Collector's Edition of the John F. Kennedy Center Program/ Magazine." Produced for the Kennedy Center by *Saturday Review*, New York: 1971.